95 Reasons NOT to Go to College

Θ

THERAN PRESS

THERAN PRESS IS THE ACADEMIC PUBLISHING IMPRINT OF SILVER GOAT MEDIA.

THERAN IS DEDICATED TO AUTHENTIC PARTNERSHIPS WITH OUR ACADEMIC ASSOCIATES,
TO THE QUALITY DESIGN OF ASCHOLARLY BOOKS, AND TO ELITE STANDARDS OF PEER REVIEW.

THERAN SEEKS TO FREE INTELLECTUALS FROM THE CONFINES OF TRADITIONAL PUBLISHING.

THERAN SCHOLARS ARE AUTHORITIES AND REVOLUTIONARIES IN THEIR RESPECTIVE FIELDS.

THERAN ENCOURAGES NEW MODELS FOR GENERATING AND DISTRIBUTING KNOWLEDGE.

FOR OUR CREATIVES. FOR OUR COMMUNITIES. FOR OUR WORLD.

WWW.THERANPRESS.ORG

This book was designed and produced by Silver Goat Media, LLC. Fargo, ND U.S.A.
www.silvergoatmedia.com
SGM, the SGM goat, Theran Press, and the Theran theta are trademarks of Silver
Goat Media.

Cover and Illustrations - Travis Klath © 2015
This book was typeset in Bodoni MT and Open Sans by Cady Ann Mittlestadt and Travis Klath

ISBN-10: 0985821221
ISBN-13: 978-0985821227 (Silver Goat Media)

2.0 - 170804

Printed and bound in the United States of America

95 Reasons NOT to Go to College

pedro degrasi

THERAN PRESS

For my students.

Two roads diverged in a wood, and I –
I took the one less traveled by,
And that has made all the difference.

– Robert Frost

Introduction

Congratulations! If you've just opened this book, or if you're just previewing it on Amazon, then you're one of a handful of people on the planet who has the amazing opportunity to think about going to college!

But even more congrats may be in order.

If you're in high school, or if you're just starting college, then you may also be one of the very few people who's not just thinking about going to college, but who's thinking about why they want to go to college in the first place. And that's a big deal.

I never thought about why I wanted to go to college.

That's why I wrote this book.

For me, going to college was always "just what people did." For me, there was no question *if* I was going to college. Instead, the question was always *where* I was going to college. *"Everyone has to go to college!"* It was like some kind of Natural Law.

But that's not right. It's not fair. And it's not true. Going to college isn't the only path. Going to college isn't the best way to find your life's purpose. And going to college certainly isn't the "only way to succeed." Going to college is a decision, an option, a possibility. Going to college is a *choice*.

So, I wrote this book to try to show you that there are plenty of reasons *not* to go to college. Some reasons are more serious than others. Some reasons will matter to you. Some won't. Regardless, I hope that this little book will help you and your family think hard about what will be one of biggest *decisions* of your life. Enjoy!

p.s. Of course, there are also a ton of reasons why you *should* go to college. (And you've probably heard most of them already.) So I've included the only one that I think matters.

How to Use This Book

The most important thing you can do when you start thinking about going to college is this: *You've got to think about going to college.* Pretty easy, right? But you'd be surprised how many smart people don't think about what they're doing– or why they're doing it. Your parents went to college. Your brothers and sisters went to college. All your friends are going to college. So that means that you should go to college, too, right? Maybe that's true. Maybe it's not. And that question is what this book is all about. It's about helping you see that going to college is a choice. So, if you want to get the most out of this book, then you'll have to do one thing: *You'll have to think for yourself.*

"But what do I think about, exactly?"

That's where I can help. I've pulled together some pretty good reasons for you to think twice about going to college. Maybe college is right for you. Maybe it's not. Regardless, if you take the time to go through this book, then you might learn something about American colleges, something about the "industry of higher education," and, hopefully, something about yourself. These issues have been discussed by scholars and educators for years. But students – the people that college is supposed to be about – have never been included in the conversation. That changes now.

That's all you need to know! Easy as pie! The only other suggestion that I have is this: Don't read this book alone. Grab this book and take it to a friend, a school counselor, a trusted mentor, or one of your parents. Go through it with them. They'll have important things to add. They might disagree with some of the things that I say. They might think I'm crazy! Or they might think that some of these issues are actually worth thinking about. Regardless, your decision about college will affect both you and your family, so they should be involved. You're not alone.

The Money

Everyone says that I must have a college degree to "succeed" nowadays. If that's true, then why is it so expensive for a necessity?

66 The baby boomlet, or baby boom echo group, born between 1988 and 1995, have flooded colleges with demand for a limited number of spots. Even so, college enrollment has risen by 138% over the past 40 years. This rising demand has tolerated increased costs and allowed universities to raise prices uninhibited by normal economic forces. 99

- Steve Odland, President and CEO of the Committee for Economic Development

First, you don't "need" a college degree to "succeed." That's a fact. Second, and more importantly: It's all about supply and demand. The more people think that they "need" college, the more people will apply to go to college. This allows the colleges themselves to jack up your cost. Increased demand = increased sticker price. While most colleges are "non-profits," many still follow "for profit" economics. Think about it: College is a luxury, not a necessity. And like the "need" for all luxuries, the "need for college" has been carefully crafted by marketers, branding experts, and salesmen. Get smart. You don't "need" to buy every single thing that's offered to you. Especially if it's overpriced.

How much will my four years of college actually cost? Can't I just multiply the first year's fees by four and see what I'll pay?

66 On average, tuition tends to increase about 8% per year. An 8% college inflation rate means that the cost of college doubles every nine years. For a baby born today, this means that college costs will be more than three times current rates when the child matriculates in college. 99

     – Finaid.org

When you begin to consider college, the nice, attractive recruiter who calls your home will sell you on a price. The first year's price. By your last year – after you've been "locked into the system" – you will pay, on average, about 30% more. Think about it like a car: The sticker price says $10,000. But you will really pay $13,000 and the salesman isn't going to tell you that when you buy. So you'll need to ask the person trying to recruit you if they can guarantee the first year's price for four years. If the answer is yes, then get it in writing. If the answer is no, then get ready to pay.

I'm a good student. Will academic scholarships make my four years of college tuition more manageable?

66 . . . the pride of winning a scholarship obscures for many students a tough reality: Getting that scholarship renewed for your whole college career isn't a sure thing. Every year, tens of thousands of rising sophomores, juniors, and seniors lose scholarships they had counted on. A MONEY analysis of financial aid reports for the 2012-2013 academic year found that colleges, on average, award merit-based scholarships to 25% of their freshmen. However, only 20% of sophomores, juniors, and seniors get similar grants. At some schools, the scholarship drop-off is much more significant. 99

– Jacob Davidson, TIME

Sometimes, an academic scholarship is like bait: a nice, juicy worm designed to bring in a nice, juicy fish. That fish, my friend, is you. This is one of the reasons why some colleges give more aid to incoming students and why there are very few new financial aid opportunities for more advanced students. Once their "fresh catch" is in the net, a school can reanalyze the financials and see whose scholarship money they can cut. Think about it: If you've made tons of new friends, met some cool teachers, and settled into your new college town, then you won't want to leave, will you? And that means you'll pay more to stay. Colleges know this about you. Don't doubt it.

Some schools are way more expensive than others. Should I sacrifice my first choice of college for a better price tag?

66 More than three-quarters of current college freshmen were admitted to their first-choice schools, according to a recently released survey from the University of California at Los Angeles, but only 56.9 percent chose to attend, an all-time low for the annual survey. Students cited high costs and lack of financial aid as the reasons they declined their top schools. 99

– Barbara Kantrowitz, The Hechinger Report

Should you give up your number one choice because of how much it costs? It depends on what your first choice is. The Ivy League and some of the top tech colleges (MIT, Stanford, etc.) can be worth the extra money in terms of their "network value" and their brand. But if your first choice is a small, expensive school that nobody has ever heard of, then you should reconsider. Think about it: Does it matter that you went to St. Olaf College if you graduate with $100,000 of debt and no one knows what an "Ollie" is? If you've got to go to college – and remember: you don't – then think hard about what you're actually paying for when you make your list of schools.

Public universities are cheaper, right?

" States have cut the amount they spend on higher education, per student, by nearly 11 percent since 2010 to the lowest level since the 1980s, according to the State Higher Education Executive Officers organization. [This has forced] the rest to be made up through higher tuition. One result is that the cost of attending community college rose nearly 9 percent this year, on average– and a significantly larger proportion of students have had to rely on federal financial aid. "

– Jon Marcus, The Hechinger Report

Public school used to be more affordable. But the costs are rising – fast. So if you're counting on a public university as the answer, then you need to look hard at the question. The value of a public degree – in terms of quality of education, name recognition, and brand value – will sometimes be less than a more expensive, private school. So you may be paying more and more for what may be an inferior product. Think about it for a moment: Why would you pay the price of a Ferrari to drive a Chevy?

My family does pretty well. They've been saving for my college education my whole life. Will they be able to pay the Estimated Family Contribution on my FAFSA form? In other words: Can my family really afford to send me to college?

> " Consider a family of four, earning $100,000 in income and having $50,000 in savings. The E.F.C. says that this family will contribute $17,375 each year to a child's college expenses. A $100,000 income translates into take-home pay of about $6,311 monthly. An E.F.C. of $17,375 means the family must contribute about $1,500 a month – every month for four years. But cutting family expenses by 25 percent every month is unrealistic. "
>
> – Steve Cohen, co-author of "Getting In: The Zinch Guide to College Admissions & Financial Aid in the Digital Age"

Can your family afford college? Probably not. But they will try anyway, because they love you. Think about it like this: Let's say you make $500 a month at your part-time job. With that money, you pay your bills. You *need* the 500 bucks to do everything that you have to do. Now, pretend that you have $375 – and that you *still* need to do everything that you used to do with $500. Can you do it? Probably not. But you can take out a loan. And that's when it gets even more expensive. Ask your recruiter to run the numbers for you and then triple check them with your family. Remember, it's not just about you.

What about school supplies? They'll probably cost more than a ruler, an eraser, and a couple of pencils, right? How much are the "extras" going to cost me?

> " The College Board reports that in 2010-2011, students could expect to spend an average of $1,137 on textbooks and supplies. A new financial accounting textbook can cost $150 to $200. "
>
> – Carole Walters, Flat World Knowledge

How much for extras? Do the math, my friend. When you do, you'll discover that you're going to pay around $4,000 extra for "supplies" over four years of college. That's on top of tuition and room and board. And since "supplies" aren't part of the "sticker price," you can get into some serious debt before you've even stepped foot into a classroom. If you think that the cost of college is just the tuition, then you need to think again.

When it comes to paying back my college loans, there are lots of options. I like the sound of cheaper monthly payments for 30 years. It sounds way better than having to make huge monthly payments for ten. Why doesn't everyone do that?

66 The $23,000 average student loan typically ends up costing around $33,000 if you include an 8% annual interest and a ten-year repayment timeline. But if that loan is consolidated to make the individual payments more manageable, the repayment period is extended to 30 years, and suddenly that original loan of $23,000 can cost the graduate about $60,000 before it's paid off. 99

– Chris Bowyer, Forbes contributor

Think about your college loans like your car again. You thought that your ride was going to cost you $10,000. But it really costs you about $30,000, because you didn't stop for two seconds to read the fine print on the loan. If you can't afford college at $15,000 a year, then what makes you think that you can afford it at $45,000 a year? Get smart. (And don't forget, the cost per year will go up every year, too.) If you have to borrow, then pay it back as fast as you can. But why borrow at all?

There are a lot of "super seniors" in college. Five years to graduate? Six? Why does it take so long to finish school?

> Today's truly 'traditional' college path is a goulash of enrollment patterns -- frequent starts and stops, serial transfers, and oscillation between full- and part-time student status. [...] Fluidity is the defining characteristic of today's college student. Things promise to get only more fluid as the recession forces more people to consider lower-cost alternatives like community colleges and part-time status.
>
> – Neil Swidey, The Boston Globe

Why does it take so long for some people to get their degree? Easy answer. It's all about the money. Lots of people, just like you, start college thinking that they understand what college costs. But guess what? They don't. So they stop taking classes, they work, and they save. And then they start up again and give their school their hard-earned loot. But since the price of college is still going up every year, they have to work and save even more to keep going to school. This can get slow. Think about it: Why work like a dog and then give someone *else* your money? Why not invest your money? Save your money? Work in a field in which you can move forward from the very beginning? Taking five or six or seven years to finish college is expensive, dangerous, and not-so-smart.

It seems like there are tons of donations to colleges from super wealthy folks. If that's the case, then why is the cost of college still rising?

> The shift away from public funding of institutions has continued, with most of the new money in higher education coming from tuition and fees, private gifts, grants, and contracts. Much of the new revenue is restricted by the donor, and is not available to pay for core educational programs.
>
> – Delta Cost Project, 2008

The guys with the big bucks don't always want their money to go to students. Sometimes, those guys want to see their names on buildings and stadiums. Remember, you're unknown to them. Many donors give to scholarship funds, of course. But the big money pulled in by college advancement offices is often aimed at "bricks and mortar" – buildings and facilities – not brains and ideas. A building is a sure thing. But you? You're a risk. And only the most enlightened kind of investor will put their money into the risk that is an educated mind. Think about it: Why would a college ask a donor to pay for you, when they could ask *you* to pay for you? You bear all the risk and the college takes all the reward. The vast majority of big donors care about "students," but they don't care about *you*, individually. Why would they?

The Recruiters

The recruiters who're calling me are getting pretty personal. They know a lot about me, especially the things I'm worried about. What's the deal?

66 Kaplan University also encourages its recruiters to focus on pain and fear. This is a page from a manual dated July 8, 2009. [...] At the bottom, in big capital, bold letters is the takeaway message for staff. *'It is all about uncovering their pain and fears. Once they are reminded of how bad things are, this will create a sense of urgency to make this change.* 99

– U.S. Senator Tom Harkin

Recruiting techniques are the definition of personal. "Uncovering *their* pain and fears," eh? Who is the "they" in this sentence? You are, my friend. Think about it: If you're afraid, then you're not thinking clearly. If you're not thinking clearly, then you're not making the best choices. Recruiters want to sell you *the idea* that you *must*, at all costs, go to college – their college. "If you don't, then you won't be successful." Or, "If you don't, then your friends will judge you." Or, "If you don't, then you'll spend your whole life flipping burgers." This culture of fear is *created* by some recruiters to keep you nervous. Because if you're edgy, then you're not thinking clearly. Then they can step in like superheroes and solve the problem for you – a problem that *they created*.

Some of these recruiters make it sound too good to be true. Are they telling me the straight story?

> " Recruiters [have] told people with felony criminal records that pursuing a criminal justice degree would allow them to achieve their dreams of joining the FBI -- an impossible scenario, because the Bureau is barred from hiring people who have been convicted of such offenses. They [have] convinced students with no access to a computer or Internet that they could use the local library for classes, even though they would need to save files and download specific software to access coursework. "
>
> – Chris Kirkham, Huffington Post

The straight story? You kidding? The recruiter is *not* your friend. He or she is a *salesperson*. Keep that truth right in front of you. Always. You're a free-swimming fish. The recruiter is the fisherman. They don't want you in the ocean. They want you in their net. (And not in anyone else's.) Many will say whatever they need to say in order to hook you. Take a second and think about what you read in "The Money." You're worth *a lot* of cash. You're a *golden* fish. Don't get caught in a net of silly lies.

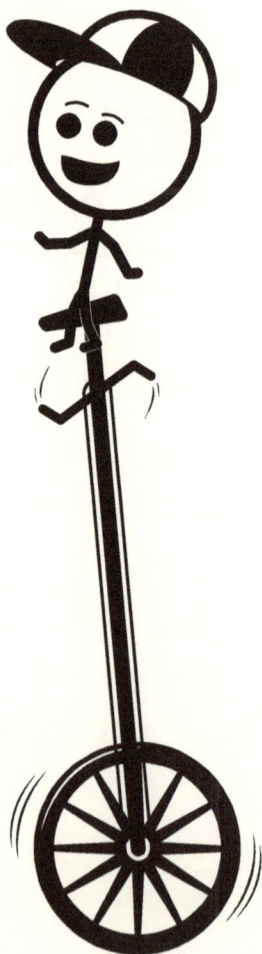

What are admissions officers looking for in terms of a "well-rounded college applicant?"

" Good colleges are not looking for the well-rounded *kid*; they're looking for the well-rounded *class*. That means they want a few super-scholars for each academic department, top athletes for each team, wonderful musicians, dancers, actors, and journalists. And they also want diversity: racial, economic, [and] geographic. "

– Michael Muska, Brooklyn's Poly Prep and co-author of Getting In!

Recruiters want a "well-rounded class," not a "well-rounded applicant." What this really means is that they want a "well-rounded crop." For a recruiter, you are a seed in that crop. A seed that they want turn into a plant to grow, cut, and sell. Not every student is a rock star. And that's just how recruiters like it. Because their primary objective is to bring in tuition dollars – *your* dollars. Think about it: If a college has to pay superstar athletes a bunch of scholarship money, then where does the money come from? Sometimes, it comes from "well-rounded students" who get a tiny scholarship and then pay full price for the rest of their tuition. Well-rounded students just like you.

Aren't athletes getting recruited super early nowadays? Even if they aren't qualified academically?

66 In today's sports world, students are offered full scholarships before they have taken their first College Boards, or even the Preliminary SAT exams. Coaches at colleges large and small flock to watch 13- and 14-year-old girls who they hope will fill out their future rosters. This is happening despite N.C.A.A. rules that appear to explicitly prohibit it. 99

– Nathaniel Popper, The New York Times

Do athletes get recruited early? You bet. But *why*? Here's one reason: Some schools don't care that much about educating you. Some care more about *rankings*. So if you're not a super student or a star athlete, then you may be a sheep. A sheep ready to be sheared so that the "super elite" can get paid to go to college – even if they really aren't that smart. Think about it for second: How and why does a football player with well-below-average scores earn an "academic" scholarship?

I've got a little saved up for college, but not much. Will my – or my family's – incomes affect how a recruiter reviews my application?

> 66 Today, more and more college admission officers want – and need – to know whether the kid can pay full-freight. And if there is a choice between two virtually-identical applicants – one who needs financial aid and one who doesn't – [then] the fat envelope is going to go to the kid who can pay full tuition. 99
>
>   – Steve Cohen, co-author of Getting In: The Zinch Guide to College Admissions & Financial Aid in the Digital Age

Pay attention to this one. Some recruiters will offer you a "financial aid package." Unless it's a full ride, you need to do the math and then ask: "Who is really paying who here?" If you aren't getting tons of financial aid, then you might also need to ask: "Am I getting into this college because I'm good? Or because I can afford to pay?" Regardless, watch out for those fishermen! Sometimes that scholarship is just another hook.

I want to attend a diverse university, but *every* school claims that they are super "diverse" when they talk to me about coming. Is this for real?

66 [Researchers] discovered that diversity, as depicted in the brochures, was over-represented. 'When we looked at African-Americans in those schools that were predominantly white, the actual percentage in those campuses was only about 5 percent of the student body. They were photographed at 14.5 percent.' 99

    – Tim Pippert, Augsberg College

More marketing. More nonsense. Institutions of higher learning are supposed to be about finding the truth, right? And yet, they will *triple* the perceived "diversity percentage" on their campus by way of carefully crafted messages. Think about it: People of color currently comprise approximately 39% of the population, and are projected to comprise approximately 57% by 2060. *Diversity is the future.* So how does a school dominated by whites pretend to be ready for the future? They pretend to be diverse. Don't believe for a second that you'll really see thousands of happy, smiling black folks and Latinos when you walk onto most campuses. Take a look at the publications. Is that the same student of color in every, single picture?

Those personalized mailers and birthday cards that I keep getting from college recruiters have got to be pricey. What are colleges spending to sell me their education?

> 66 On average, a college or university spends about $585 to recruit each applicant, $806 to recruit each admitted student and $2,408 to recruit each enrolled student. 99
>
> – William M. Chace, former president of Wesleyan University and of Emory University

You are Big Business. Some recruiters won't just tell you what you want to hear. They'll also try – really hard – to make you feel "special." Those fancy cards and nice on-campus lunches all have one objective: to get you enrolled so that you and your family can start paying. So if your recruiter is talking about giving you serious money, and if you have it in writing, then that's great! Otherwise, all the cards, emails, and happy faces in the world don't mean one damn thing.

I'm worth way more than my GPA and my SAT show. There's so much more to me than a bunch of scores. What's the deal with these "admissions criteria?" Why do colleges care so much about these numbers?

66 The tests we rely on so heavily really don't measure creative thinking and they don't measure common sense thinking, wisdom, ethics, work ethic – they don't measure your character. [...] Admissions should be based on the mission of your college or university. It changes the kids who are accepted and it begins to change how you think about what it means to have a talented student. 99

– Robert Sternberg, Cornell University

Colleges care about your SAT and your GPA because they are "measurable" and "quantifiable" data. These data give them a sense of control. These data are based on the idea that "education" is an "industry." Think about it: Colleges want high SAT scores so that they can raise the averages of their incoming classes. They want to raise the averages of their incoming classes so that their Board Members and Presidents think that the recruiters are doing a good job bringing in a smart "crop." But once the crop is in, they dump all the incoming students into the *same* machine and crank out the *same* "polished," "well-rounded," and "well-educated" graduates. So, what does your SAT score really mean? *Nada*.

Are big-shot high school athletes sometimes bribed by recruiters to come to schools?

> The Bag Man excuses himself to make a call outside, on his 'other phone,' to arrange delivery of $500 in cash to a visiting recruit. The player is rated No. 1 at his position nationally and is on his way into town. We're sitting in a popular restaurant near campus almost a week before National Signing Day, talking about how to arrange cash payments for amateur athletes.
>
> – Steven Godfrey, SBNation

Yes.

Why do recruiters fight so hard? Do they have quotas to fill or something?

66 At smaller institutions, even a margin of 10 paying students could be the difference between operating in the black or in the red. 99

– Barmak Nassirian, American Association of State Colleges and Universities

Are you starting to see how important you are to colleges and universities? They *need* you. Especially the small ones. That's why recruiters are working so hard for your attention. *They* need *you*. But does that necessarily mean that *you* need *them*? Think about it: Why all the special consideration? Why all the nice cards and messages and phone calls? Why the campus visits and overnight stays with the cool kids? Because they want to educate you? Sure. But they also want your money. The survival of many of these institutions is tied directly to whether you say "Yes" or "No." So bargain like you're a star quarterback, OK?

The "Student-Athlete"

College sports make *tons* of money. Into whose pockets do those dollars flow?

> 66 Hundreds of millions of dollars of advertising revenue will pour into (CBS) as a result of this year's men's college basketball tournament, commonly referred to as "March Madness." Last year's tournament brought in $613 million in advertising to the broadcast company, second only to the Super Bowl. But the athletes responsible for the spectacle receive no financial gain from the contracts, and in fact often live below the federal poverty line. 99
>
> – Joey LeMay, MintPress

College sports make piles of loot. That's why, in the eyes of most college coaches and athletic recruiters, student-athletes are like thoroughbred horses. They should be strong, fast, and cheap. And, like race horses, college athletes will be systematically exploited. Think about it: You love your sport. You want to live the dream. You get a $25,000 scholarship to play. And then your college makes *millions* off you. The perfect scam.

How does playing college sports affect athletes' mental and physical health later in life?

66 After players leave the game, many suffer from chronic traumatic encephalopathy, or CTE. The incurable, degenerative disease has a number of pernicious effects, including depression, memory loss, and difficulty controlling emotion. Repeated concussions damage the brain's executive function – the part of our mind responsible for rationality and goal-oriented behavior. Needless to say, being emotionally unstable, unable to plan for the future, and incapable of remembering things is a hard and painful way to live, and sadly, many are simply unable to bear up under the strain. A recent spate of suicides among former football players have been linked to CTE. 99

> – Jeff Fecke, Care 2

Later in life, playing college sports can cost you. You don't get paid to play – because you love it. You sacrifice your body to play – because you love it. You take hits for the team – because you love it. And at the end of the day, you may have *twice* the medical expenses of a non-athlete. And the college makes a killing. Think about it: You might have a passion for sports. But does that mean that you have to sell your body to your school so *they* can profit from *your* dreams?

Why aren't student-athletes getting punished when they screw up?

> " Our athletes are the closest things we have in this country to gods. In a nation devoid of royalty and a world in which superheroes only exist in comic books and big budget movies, it's our sports figures who represent the pinnacle of perfection, the American ideal of strength and grace. And when that narrative doesn't work, when instead an athlete is accused of something as monstrous as sexual assault, too often it's easier to ignore the unpleasant possibilities than investigate their merit. "
>
> – Mary Elizabeth Williams, Salon

When athletes get into trouble, colleges get into trouble – financial trouble. Think about it: If you're making millions on star athletes, and if your athletes are in jail, then how can you keep making money? You can't. Is that fair? No. Is that right? No. But that's college athletics.

Our society places a ton of pressure on young people to be "thin and fit." How does this affect student-athletes whose *job* is to be "thin and fit?"

> A study of Division 1 NCAA athletes found that more than one-third of female athletes reported attitudes and symptoms placing them at risk for anorexia nervosa. [...] Though most athletes with eating disorders are female, male athletes are also at risk–especially those competing in sports that tend to emphasize diet, appearance, size and weight. In weight-class sports and aesthetic sports about 33% of male athletes are affected. In female athletes in weight class and aesthetic sports, disordered eating occurs at estimates of up to 62%.
>
> – National Eating Disorders Association

College sports are supposed to be about physical and mental health. But that's not always how it works out — especially when colleges link scholarship dollars to "performance" and "appearance." Think about it for a second: Is it really worth destroying your body for a few thousand dollars? Isn't your body worth more than that? It's the only one you've got, after all!

I've seen some *really* bad students get to start in the big game Friday night. They can't pass algebra, but they're campus heroes? What the heck is going on?

> 66 College presidents have put in jeopardy the academic credibility of their universities just so we can have this entertainment industry. ... The NCAA continually wants to ignore this fact, but they are admitting students who cannot read. College textbooks are written at the ninth-grade level, so we are putting these elite athletes into classes where they can't understand the textbooks. Imagine yourself sitting in a class where nothing makes sense. 99
>
> – Gerald Gurney, University of Oklahoma

Jocks are protected because the money machine needs to be fueled. Colleges throw these "student-athletes" into the grinder and then let them kill themselves on the field for the school and the team. These students don't get paid, some don't even get taught. Professors will sometimes make "academic exceptions" in these classes, for the "good of the college." But at the end of the day, many elite athletes will exit college barely more prepared for life than when they started. And that's b*ll$h!t.

Why aren't college athletes paid for their skill and their work?

> " Imagine you're an English scholar. You write a novel that becomes a best seller, but have to forfeit any profit to the school because you're already taken care of with paid expenses. Or what if you're a talented engineering student who builds something as innovative as Facebook in a dorm room, but couldn't reap any benefits, because you were told the college experience is enough? "
>
> – Greg Johnson, The Daily Targum

Student-athletes don't get paid because the colleges don't have to pay them. The NCAA by-laws forbid it. If colleges *did* have to pay their student-athletes, then all those millions (and billions) of dollars in profits that some colleges see every year would vanish in a puff of smoke. And when players actually try to fight for their rights, they're crushed by administrations, coaches, and attorneys. Think about it: In this rigged system, colleges have everything to gain when they don't pay their student-athletes. And student-athletes have everything to lose.

How much are college coaches getting paid?

66 The numbers are mind-boggling: according to USA Today, salaries of new head football coaches at the bowl-eligible schools increased by 35% from 2011 to 2012. Average annual pay has ballooned to $1.64 million, an astonishing increase of more than 70% since 2006. This is all as tuition hikes, furloughs, layoffs and cuts in student aid have continued unabated. In an era of stagnating wages, compensation for coaching a college football team has risen like a booster's adrenaline during bowl season. 99

– Dave Zirin, The Nation

College coaches make serious bank. And who pays for all of this? Usually, it's you. The typical student. Why are your fees going up? Why do you pay more for books? Why does your dorm room cost so much? If you think college sports don't have something to do with it, then you're wrong. Wake up. Do you want to go to college to get educated, to get prepared, and to explore your mind? Or do you want to pay for some fat-cat coach to exploit his "student-athletes" and get rich?

College games are huge productions. How much are universities spending on athletics?

> 66 The Knight Commission says Division I schools with football spent $91,936 per athlete in 2010, seven times the spending per student of $13,628. Division I universities without football spent $39,201 per athlete, more than triple the average student spending. Nearly every university loses money on sports. Even after private donations and ticket sales, they fill the gap by tapping students paying tuition or state taxpayers. Athletics is among the biggest examples of the eruption in spending by universities that has experts concerned about whether higher education can sustain itself. 99
>
> – Cliff Peale, The Cincinnati Enquirer

Read Mr. Peale's quote. Now, read it again. For schools with big athletic programs, do you really think that college is about *your* education? Money talks and b*ll$h!t walks. These are *facts*. If you're going to be attending a Division I school, then you need to know the truth. Don't give in and say: "That's just the way it is." It's this way because of individual choices. Choices like yours.

"Amateur" vs. "Pro." Where does the student-athlete fall?

> The term 'student-athlete' was deliberately ambiguous. College players were not students at play (which might understate their athletic obligations), nor were they just athletes in college (which might imply they were professionals). That they were high-performance athletes meant they could be forgiven for not meeting the academic standards of their peers; that they were students meant they did not have to be compensated, ever, for anything more than the cost of their studies. Student-athlete became the NCAA's signature term, repeated constantly in and out of courtrooms.
>
> – Taylor Branch, "The Shame of College Sports," The Atlantic

"Student-athletes" aren't "amateurs" and they aren't "pros." In fact, the term "student-athlete" itself is a racket. You can see that, right? The whole machine is designed to make money for colleges on the backs of "student-athletes." The NCAA, the colleges, the boosters, the donors, the administration – all of them – will do almost *anything* to preserve the status quo. Think about it: You run a factory. The factory makes you money. But you never have to pay the workers. Would you *ever* want this situation to change?

There seems to be a lot of corruption in college sports. It's been going on for a long time. How can it continue this way? Who's at fault?

> " Why is the apple core rotten? That's the crucial question at the heart of the matter. Why is college football so messed up? A system that not only encourages corruption but also thrives off it is not the problem. Universities, hypocritical sausage factories of spin though they may be, are not the problem. Money is not the problem. The problem at the beating heart of college football is you. And the problem is me. Fans of the game are fueling this insane and backward beast that college football has become. It's bad, but we don't care. Give us more. That quarter pounder with cheese is cheap and tasty. That menthol cigarette goes down smooth. The BCS system exploits the poor, but the rich love it. Every Saturday in the fall is an excuse to party. "
>
> – Joseph Goodman, Miami Herald

Individual choices are important. They define societies. They define lives. The choices that *you* make count. So, when it comes time to make a choice, you need to *think* about it, and you need to think about it hard. *You create your own destiny.* Your courage, creativity, and commitment are the things that will move you forward. So do the right thing: *think*.

The Student Customer

I've been touring a ton of campuses. I'm pretty amazed by some of the perks and amenities. They sure make it easy for me to move away from home, don't they?

66 A free movie theater. A 25 person hot tub and spa with a lazy 99 river and whirlpool. A leisure pool with biometric hand scanners for secure entry. A 50 foot climbing wall to make exercise interesting. And a top-of-the-line steak restaurant with free, five course meals. This isn't a list of items from a resort brochure. They're facilities you can find on a college campus. And with college construction costs rising, it could be the best four-year getaway you've ever had.

– Cara Newlon, Forbes

Most colleges want you to leave home – and to be super comfortable when you do it. Thus, the *campus-as-spa* phenomenon. The campus-spa has become more and more popular in the last twenty years. This is because campus recruiters are no longer selling you just an "education." They're selling you an "experience." This can be good. But it can also be pretty bad. If you're paying by the class, then why does so much of your money go to hot tubs and steak restaurants? These perks don't prepare you for the future. They do, however, illustrate what colleges will do to attract your tuition dollars: anything.

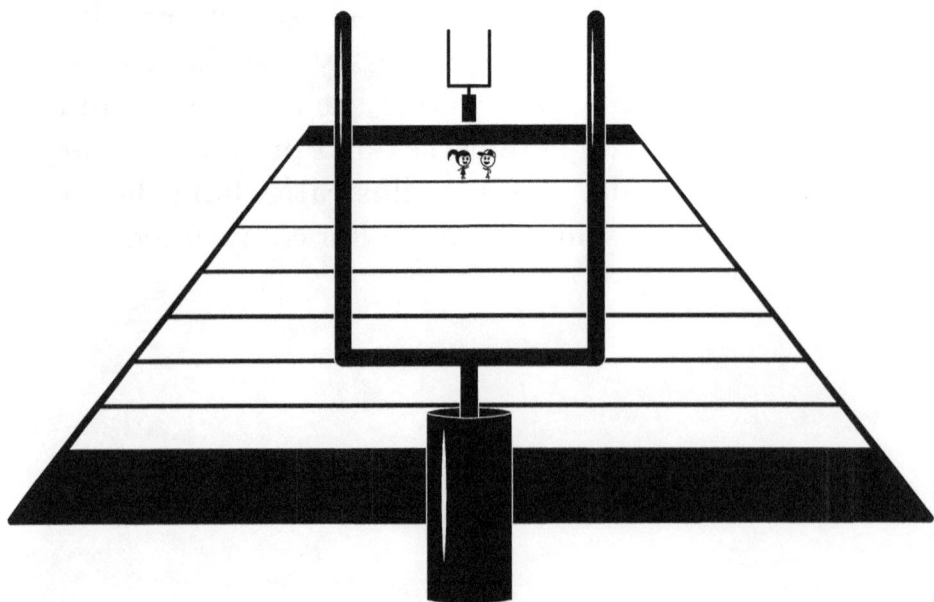

Am *I* paying for all these perks and amenities that colleges are offering me?

> 66 Take a look at what Harvard University promotes on the first page of its college admissions brochure: 'You can fit a football field in the clean room of the Laboratory for Integrated Science and Engineering.' While a school's resources are important, the fact that Harvard University takes the time to detail the vast expanse of its amenities [...] in the first few pages of its brochure shows just how significant they are to a college's image. What brochures don't tell you is that these extensive amenities are covered by the rising college tuition. This is especially true for public universities, where tuition covers nearly half of their revenue. 99

> – Matthew Segal, co-founder of OurTime.org

You pay for all these "luxuries" with your tuition. This is one of the reasons why fees and course costs have gone up so fast in the last twenty years. That's ironic because tuition is billed by the credit hour. How many "credit hours" is a giant food court worth? Or a new climbing wall? Or a mega huge fitness complex? If you're paying by the class, then why doesn't most of your money go towards bettering your classes?

Do all these extra perks and amenities have an effect on colleges' academics?

66 The 'resortification' of colleges also encourages students to view themselves as customers, and instructors as retail workers employed to serve them. The 'A' is now the most common grade on college campuses nationwide; it accounts for roughly 43% of all grades given. 99

– Nick Romeo, The Daily Beast contributor

If in today's college, you are a customer, and if the customer is always right, then how can you fail? Easy: *you can't*. The down side? Your grades are basically worthless. Your professor doesn't have the time to deal with the two hundred other students she teaches each year, so she will take the easy road and give you the grade that you want, not the grade you deserve. You've paid your tuition. And you've bought your "A." And now you get to go eat a five-course dinner. But stop and think about it for a second: Do you really want to *buy* your "A?" Don't you want to *earn* it?

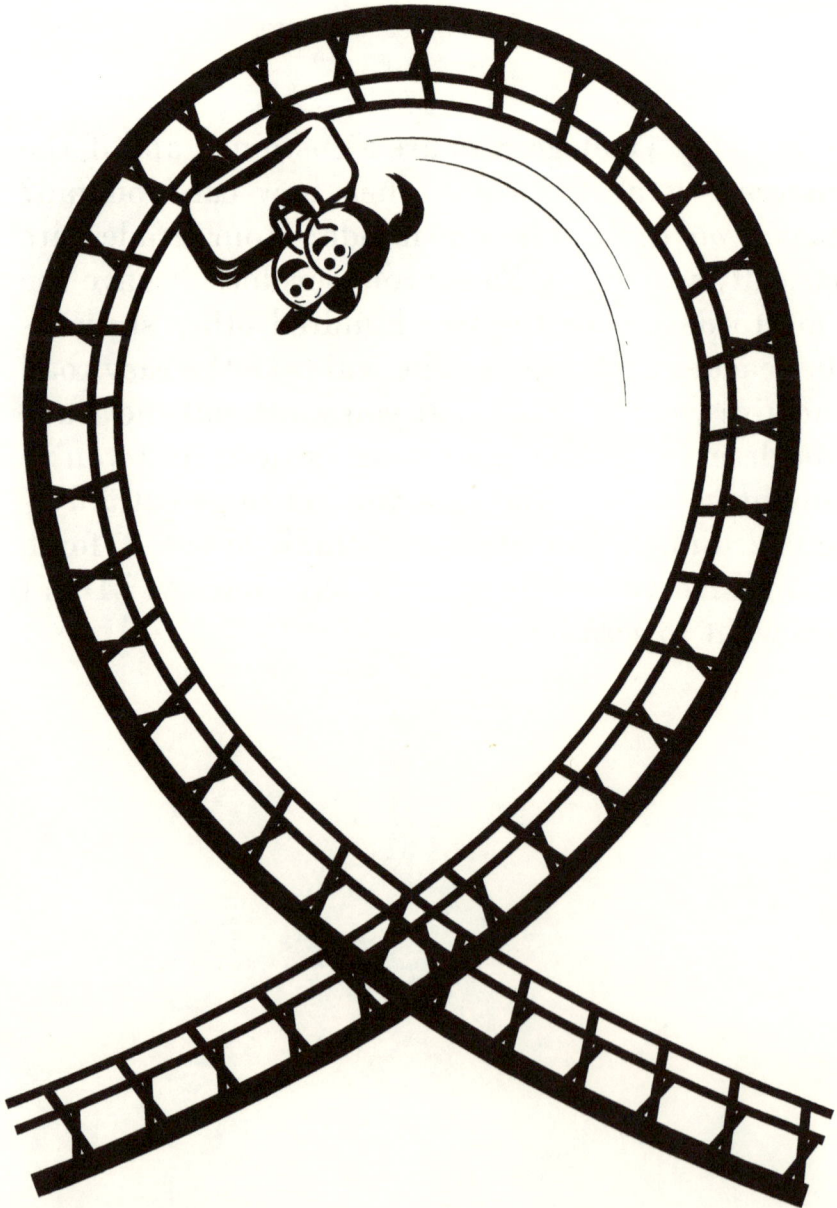

I've seen some *insane* dining centers during campus tours. Aren't college students supposed to be starving?

> " Every date's a cheap one at High Point, where, in addition to the on-campus movie theater (that shows first-run features) with complimentary snacks, roaming ice cream truck, and multiple swimming pools/hot tubs dotting the pristine campus, this NC school boasts its own fancy steak house – as in 'no jeans allowed' fancy – at which students indulge in a weekly, three-course meal of filet mignon, seared duck breast, etc. Yep, with their dining points. "
>
> – Sophie-Clare Hoeller, Thrillist

Food is a big deal. Who doesn't like a nice, big, juicy meal? Everybody does! And colleges know this. That's the reason why many will take you to their dining facilities, right off the bat, during your first campus tour. (Those visits also make your parents feel good, since they can see – firsthand – how "well taken care of" you'll be at your new home.) If you decide that you like this kind of luxury, then enjoy it! But remember: You'll be paying for it for the next thirty years.

Are all these colleges really trying to sell their campus to me? Or are they all just "trying to keep up with the Joneses?"

> " If everyone has a climbing wall and a new recreation center and serves sushi, then it doesn't become a marketing advantage, it just becomes something you do to avoid falling behind everyone else. And I think that's happening. "
>
> – James Garland, former president of Miami University

One of the problems with colleges spending tons of money on climbing walls, hot tubs, and sushi bars is that these projects often keep money away from professors, research, and scholarships. In other words, these gimmick projects can keep colleges from spending money on your education. Some colleges are so worried about getting you in the door, that they will actually sacrifice their purpose (and their academic integrity) just to get you enrolled. And since many colleges are doing it, the amount of money pulled away from your education will continue to rise.

I'm really sold on these cool, new classes. I can learn about philosophy and Star Trek, or history and Harry Potter, or sociology and the Hunger Games. Those are so much cooler than Psychology 101, right?

> In an increasingly business-like world of higher education, appealing to high school seniors with a hip course catalog brings in more applications, which allows a school to be choosier, which in turn gives a university a higher selectivity ranking – a hot commodity in a fiercely competitive industry.
>
> – Karlee Weinmann, Business Insider

It isn't just cool facilities that colleges use to get you signed up and in the door – it's also cool classes. Why take Algebra, when you can take *The History of Middle Earth*? Why take Chemistry, when you can take *Gender and Class Inequality at Hogwarts*? Those sound fun, no doubt. But what're you really going to *get* out of them? Think about it for a second: Do you really think that your employer cares that you can name all the dwarves in Bilbo's company? Or that you know the intimate details of Snape's family history? Heck no. So consider carefully what's showing up on your transcript. It's going to be around for a long time.

I've been accepted to four different universities. All of a sudden, it's like several different stores are vying for my business. Why is everyone trying so hard to woo me?

66 More applications mean plummeting acceptance rates – less than 10 percent at many elite institutions. Those odds only encourage teens to hedge their bets by applying to more schools. When they get into several, it's then the colleges' turn to do the lobbying. [...] It's time to roll out the red carpet. Boston University is inviting some students for breakfast with a dean. Columbia is dangling a night tour of New York City, and Wilkes University, a private institution in Wilkes-Barre, Pa., put its mascot, 'the Colonel,' and 30 of its students on a bus to dazzle prospects, said college consultant Katherine Cohen, founder of IvyWise.com. The University of Chicago, which has seen applications more than double in the past five years to 21,669 this year, sent all prospective students a maroon scarf following their acceptance letters. 99

– Bonnie Miller Rubin and Jodi S. Cohen, Chicago Tribune

We talked a little bit about these sales tactics when we discussed "The Recruiters." The *campus-spa* is part of that same pattern. Colleges will do anything (and say anything) to get you onto their campuses and into their enrollment. And you pay for their efforts. Think about that for a second: *You* are paying *them* to recruit *you*.

Every time I go on a campus tour, the guides really focus on showing me the wellness centers. Why are these buildings getting more focus than libraries or academic centers?

> For roughly the price of a single Gulfstream G650 jet, the Athletics and Events Center at Ithaca College in upstate New York opened in 2011 for all students. Highlights include a 130,000-square-foot field house, an aquatics pavilion with an Olympic-sized swimming pool (where students can take classes like aquatic Zumba [you know you want to]) and a multisport outdoor stadium with a field that lights up in case you can't sleep at 3 a.m. and feel like getting into some Ultimate Frisbee.
>
> – Jordan Zirm, Stack

If colleges are going to stuff you full of yummy food in their campus dining centers, then they better give you an awesome place to work it off! On average, 70% of students that enroll in college will gain between 8-11 pounds of body fat over their time on campus. (All-you-can-eat buffets take their toll!) So, to offset this reality, colleges will often stress the health-conscious atmosphere of their campuses. And what better way to do this than with a multi-million dollar building that *you* get to pay for?

Surely, all these perks aren't just about attracting your typical, American, over-achieving student to pick *that* college, right?

    " The awe-inspiring amenities may help some schools attract international students, who typically do pay the full posted price for their education. For one thing, they are not eligible for federal aid programs, such as Stafford and Perkins loans, or scholarships sponsored by state governments. Some schools offer need-based aid to students who are not U.S. citizens, but typically on a very limited basis. **"**

      – Doug Podolsky, U.S. News and World Report

It's a good thing to remember that these perks aren't just there for *American* citizens. Many of them are specifically designed to attract wealthy students from abroad who are willing and able to pay full cost. So if you think your campus is looking more and more like a high-priced vacation resort, then you're right. For some foreign students, that's *exactly* what it is.

Should all these perks really influence my decision of which school I go to?

66 Given the average $10,000-a-year annual tuition and fees for even a state-supported college, you might think these trifles are bit like the free cup holder that the salesman says he'll throw in if you'll buy a new car from HIM. 99

– Ted Landphair, Voice of America reporter

Making a decision about your future and your education based on the quality of a college's movie theatre or steak house is – perhaps – one of the stupidest things that you could do. But studies show that more and more students are choosing colleges based on this kind of "value." And that's what's really scary. The brainwashing is working. Costs are rising, salaries for professors are going down, but the sheep are lining up for the shearing ... just as long as they can have an all-you-can-eat dessert bar.

The Professors

Don't all professors have tenure?

66 Of all college instructors, 76 percent, or over 1 million, teach part time because institutions save a lot of money when they replace full-time, tenured faculty with itinerant teachers, better known as adjuncts. 99

    – Claudio Sanchez, NPR

No. Not all professors have tenure. According to some sources, over three-quarters of teachers teaching at the college level are actually part-timers. These folks are usually younger, less-experienced, desperate for work, and willing to do almost anything to stay connected to their academic passion or field of interest. Of course, not all adjuncts have an MFA or a PhD and not all will earn a "terminal degree." The point is that while you continue to pay *more*, the colleges are paying the people who teach you *less*. Think about it: Why hire a teacher full-time (with benefits, retirement, and a decent salary) when you could hire one at a fraction of the cost and still raise tuition?

All profs get paid well right? I mean, our childrens'
education is the future, isn't it?

66 My university pays $2,100 per class which means even if I work at
100%, 10 classes per academic year, I would only make $21,000. 99

— Anonymous, "The Just-In-Time Professor" Survey

Since many of your teachers will be part-timers,
they're actually *not* well-paid. Some of them will
be horribly paid, in fact. Some will make less per
hour than if they worked in the fast food industry.
This low pay reflects how some institutions value
their educational mission. Think about it like this:
A company spends money on things that it values.
If your college's bean counters won't pay your profs,
then what does that tell you about what they think
is truly important?

Why would a college choose to hire adjunct faculty instead of full professors?

> [...] using cheap and vulnerable labor is a business practice that goes as far back as you can trace private enterprise, and unions emerged in response. In the universities, cheap, vulnerable labor means adjuncts and graduate students. Graduate students are even more vulnerable, for obvious reasons. The idea is to transfer instruction to precarious workers, which improves discipline and control but also enables the transfer of funds to other purposes apart from education.
>
> – Noam Chomsky, Professor Emeritus of MIT

No matter what your recruiter tells you, higher education is still a *business*. Sure, many institutions are "not for profit" or "non-profit." But, as I mentioned before, many still operate on standard business models. Think about it like this: You can hire two different people to mow your yard. "Bob" costs $100 – but you have to sign a long-term contract that says he'll mow your yard until he retires. "Janet" costs $5 – and she will mow your lawn once, or twice, or forever, or never again. Which would *you* hire?

Do professors get good benefits?

66 'Benefits are really out of reach at my pay scale,' one adjunct
wrote. 'The health care plan that I could buy into costs more than
my take-home pay even on a good year (and far more than I earn
in a bad year). I don't earn enough to save for retirement (every
month is a struggle just to pay the basic bills). My 'retirement' plan
is to work until they bury me.' 99

– Colleen Flaherty, Inside Higher Ed

Sure, professors get good benefits – if they're lucky enough to have a tenure-track job. In that case, the benefits are usually like any other half-decent company. But if your teacher is only on a term contract, or if she's an adjunct, then she gets *nothing*. Adjunct gets sick? "Don't worry! Plenty more where that one came from!" (Cue evil chuckle.) Why pay all that extra loot, when you can just put it back into the "general fund?" When colleges hire adjuncts, all the money normally used to support full-time teachers stays safely in the bank.

Do all professors get the opportunity to work on their research?

> " If those scholars had been born a generation later, trapped in a lifetime of adjunct work, how much of that output would have been possible? Would they have been able to progress in their scholarship and their career? Would they have been able to create university programs, or establish world-renowned foundations? Of course not. We will never know the amount of scholarship that's been lost in this shift to casualizing the work of our professors. But if you assume even a 50% reduction in the output of a full-time faculty professor and multiply that by the 1.3 million adjuncts, you begin to get a sense of the devastation. This is an invisible cost, suffered not only by the individual scholars themselves, but by the society in which we live. "

> – Debra Leigh Scott, The Homeless Adjunct

New knowledge, new ideas, and new visions – in short: *research* – all cost money. Lots of it. But when you're in the "business of education," that money is often better spent on a new sprinkler system, or a new parking lot, or a few more administrators. Many middle and small-sized colleges don't see value in investing in great talent. Many don't actually want to be at the center of innovation. (That requires risk, courage, and leadership.) They want things to run like they've always run. So – no. Not all colleges support the research of their faculty.

Universities support their teachers with professional development, leave, and university services, right?

66 Access to university services [for teachers] is often limited: 47% received copying services less than two weeks before classes started and 45% gained library privileges two weeks before the start of class. Twenty-one percent never received any curriculum guidelines or access to office space. 99

> – Center for the Future for Higher Education, "Who is Professor 'Staff'?"

Your professors often don't get the support that they need to do their jobs. I once knew a chair of an elite philosophy department that did the secretarial work for her entire department. A world-famous expert in Sartre spending ten hours a week standing in front of a Xerox machine. Not teaching. Not writing. Not exploring the boundaries of liberty and mind. *Making flippin' copies.* Because her college thought that was a "good use of institutional resources." She begged for some help – nothing happened. Does that sound like the kind of institution where you want to be? If not, then ask your prospective teachers when you're visiting campus how well they are supported by their college.

What does this "tenure track" thing that everyone keeps talking about actually mean?

> " You enter the marathon of the first 2 years toward tenure. During this time, be prepared to work approximately 60-70 hours per week. [...] Theoretically you have the summer off. But you don't actually have the summer off. During this time, you must prepare your fall classes and do the bulk of your research and writing, because during the academic year you are too busy teaching and performing administrative service. [...] During these first years, you must simultaneously develop a stable of classes (preparing lectures, activities, assessments, and content for 2-3 new courses each semester for a while), teach a couple hundred students in about three classes per semester (whose evaluations also count toward tenure, quite a lot at a teaching university like mine), prove that you are conducting new research (i.e., go after grants and conduct research that is not repeating your dissertation), write one or more publications per year, attempt to transform your dissertation into a book [...], attend endless meetings to be in service to your university, and waste a lot more time than you'd think answering emails and filling out paperwork. "

> – Karen Kelsky, "The Professor Is In"

Going up for tenure is a blessing and a curse. On one hand, if your professor can please her university during her first seven years of employment, then she can keep her job for the rest of her life. On the other hand, those seven "trial years" are going to be so exhausting that she might not be a good professor when they're over. And since the wages for some teachers (even those that are tenured) keep dropping, she will have little incentive to keep on top of things when (if) she finally arrives at the "finish line." Sometimes, a tired, tenured prof can be worse than an adjunct.

Does the use of adjunct professors affect me as a student?

> 66 Research suggests that the inaccessibility of part-time faculty to students due [to] time pressures, lack of office space, and holding jobs at multiple locations has an inverse, negative effect on student outcomes. 99
>
> – Adrianna Kezar and Daniel Maxey, Pallias Center for Higher Education

Let's say that you're going to spend $5,000 a semester for college. For that kind of money, don't you think that you should be able to meet – to actually sit down – with your professors? If you answered "no," then congrats! You're just the kind of student that some of today's colleges love. If you answered "yes," then you *must* do your homework before you put down your deposit. Demand accountability from your recruiter. Demand the truth. How many adjuncts or teaching assistants will be teaching you during your first term of college?

Is there any job security as a professor if you don't have tenure or if you aren't on a "tenure track" line?

66 As an adjunct there is no job security. I am scheduled to teach a class at [a Boston university] in the fall. That class can be canceled up to the morning it is supposed to start – and that is it. No pay. So all of us are hustling for work. If I am offered another class and there is a conflict, I have to pick one or the other – but if the one I picked is canceled, then I lose my compensation because the other one will no longer be available. They treat us like we are Kleenex. 99

> – Anonymous, "The High Cost of Living: Boston," Adjunct Action

Sounds like working at Taco Bell might be a little safer, eh? At least there, a person gets to eat a burrito during their lunch break. And they'll probably even have a contract. This directly affects you as a student. How can you expect a teacher to commit fully to your education when your college refuses to commit to them?

Aren't college teachers able to teach whatever the heck they want?

6 6 Where the faculty lacks the protection of tenure, university administrators are free to interfere in the classroom and in the laboratory – and they do so with alacrity. Where they can, administrators will interfere with even the most meritorious academic research, publication, and communication if their results challenge the interests of important donors and constituencies or threaten administrators' own interests. 9 9

– Benjamin Ginsberg, John Hopkins University

If your teachers aren't in charge of their classes, if they aren't 100% engaged in their material, then how are they supposed to get *you* excited about it? You've got to find out the percentage of tenured faculty in any institution to which you apply. Get that percentage in writing. And if the recruiter won't help you, then ask to speak to his or her boss. Or look it up online. Do the research! It's *your* money. You want to make sure that you're going to a place where teachers are in charge of their own classes and where they have the power to do the right thing for you.

The Administrators

What's the deal with college administrations being so large? It reminds me of a huge corporation. I thought this was supposed to be a *school*? What gives?

> As university presidents have come to be more like CEO's of universities, their entourages have grown as well. Universities have come to take the look of a top-heavy bloated corporation like General Motors, with Vice-Presidents layered one atop the other. In a world of lax budget constraints owing to flush endowments, it is easier to fritter away resources on unproductive bureaucrats and internal empire-building.
>
> – Todd Zywicki, George Mason University School of Law

Administrators are like roaches. They multiply – fast and furious. And since there's usually nobody watching the money and since there's little accountability, whoever can sell themselves as a "smart and sexy leader" can come into a college, hire a dozen staff, and set up her own little empire at your expense. The people on top call this "institutional development." You should call it b*ll$h!t. Ask your recruiter what the faculty : administrator ratio is. If it's not better than 1.25 : 1, then your tuition dollars are going to pay bureaucrats, not teachers. Time to step on some roaches.

How much does an academic dean make?

" Did you know that an academic dean at a doctoral institution receives a median salary of $190,000 (plus generous fringe benefits) or that the median salary of an assistant dean is above $116,000? "

– Daniel L. Bennett, Center for College Affordability and Productivity

Isn't it interesting that the top dogs (who don't teach) make $190,000, while the adjuncts that they hire to do the *real* work make $3,000 a class? Makes you wonder, eh? If you want to make sure that your education dollars are going to your *education*, then you need to get smart. Think about it: What will the swarm of assistant deans that infest your new college really *do* for you? Easy answer: nothing. They run lame committees and silly workshops and count FTE (Full Time Employment) budgets. But far more importantly, they put out fires created by other assistant deans. They are one of the major reasons why college has gotten so expensive. They've gotta be stopped. And the only way to do it is to pull the plug on the money. *Your* money.

What does an administrator do?

66 Generally speaking, a million-dollar president could be kidnapped by space aliens and it would be weeks or even months before his or her absence from campus was noticed. 99

– Benjamin Ginsberg, The Fall of the Faculty: The Rise of the All-Administrative University and Why It Matters

Yeah. What Ben said.

54

Do you think college administrators sweep things under the rug?

> " Schools are treating sexual assault as a PR problem, as an image risk to be swept away so that, in the high-stakes games of college rankings and university branding, they don't scare off prospective students or alumni dollars. They treat survivors like liabilities to be managed, mitigated, and swept aside. "
>
> – Dana Bolger, Amherst College student

So, you might be thinking that a situation as serious as sexual assault is a place where administrators might be able to do something important. But often it's just the opposite. There are administrative positions in some colleges specifically charged with *lying* to their public, their communities, and their students. Think about it: The entire higher education industry is about *branding*. And if your "brand" looks "dangerous," then you're screwed. So instead of protecting you, some administrators are hired to protect the image of their institutions. In essence, you pay them to lie to you.

55

How are my teachers affected by the administration's power and size?

66 Before they employed an army of professional staffers, administrators were forced to rely on the cooperation of the faculty to carry out tasks ranging from admissions to planning. An administration that lost the confidence of the faculty might find itself unable to function. Today, ranks of staffers form a bulwark of administrative power in the contemporary university. These administrative staffers do not work for or, in many cases, even share information with the faculty. They help make the administration, in the language of political science, 'relatively autonomous,' marginalizing the faculty. 99

– Benjamin Ginsberg, John Hopkins University

The people you pay to educate you don't have nearly as much power over your education as you might think. Pretty scary. And it affects all aspects of your college experience. Ask your recruiter how many *layers* of administration exist within your area of interest. Do your own research. You need to be able to count the bureaucratic layers between you and the president of your new college on one hand. Anything more than that is administrative bloat. Like this: You » your professors » your department chair » an assistant dean » a dean or provost » the president. That is OK. More layers? Might be time to run away. Fast.

How much does the administration cost me as a student?

66 If the average salary and fringe benefits of these workers [non-teaching professional staff] is $75,000 a year (and many "deanlets" make vastly more than that), the costs of this increased staffing add up to about one-fourth of all tuition fees paid in 2010. No wonder tuition increases far outstrip the general inflation rate. 99

– Richard K. Vedder, Center for College Affordability and Productivity

Think about this for a second. 25%. TWENTY FIVE PERCENT of all tuition is paid to people who don't deliver any education back to you. Think about it: When you order a pizza and it shows up at your door, you expect there to be a whole pizza in the box, right? But what if your pizza box showed up and there was a giant slice of pie missing? Would you still pay for it? Yes or no? Administrators are eating your pizza.

How fast is university bureaucracy growing?

" In terms of growth, the number of full-time administrators per 100 students at America's leading universities increased by 39.3% between 1993 and 2007, while the number of employees engaged in teaching, research, or service only increased by 17.6%. "

> – Jay P. Greene, University of Arkansas

Don't you think it's interesting how this lines up with the rising costs that we talked about earlier? Think about it: Costs are way up – and the number of administrators is way up. Coincidence? Hardly. *That is your money they're spending.* And even worse: Your money is going right into the pockets of the people who are one of the main causes of this whole mess. These administrators are – quite literally – being paid to hire more people like them. And they're using your cash to do it!

How about the big dogs? What are presidents of colleges and universities paid?

> In 2013, Ohio State University President E. Gordon Gee earned $6,057,615. This, according to the Chronicle of Higher Education, made him the top paid public college leader in the country – one of nine to break the $1 million mark.
>
> – Jordan Weissmann, The Atlantic

Big salaries are not evil, by themselves. They're evil if they're not well-earned. Remember what you read nine pages ago from Ben Ginsberg? Why would you pay anyone a million dollars if they weren't doing real, true, amazing work? Real work – like holding themselves accountable? True work – like putting education before football? Amazing work – like being a leader? That's worth a million, easy. (Probably more!) But if your college president is doing anything less than amazing work, then you're probably being robbed.

You always hear about the "red tape" in government. How often do things get tied up in a college bureaucracy?

> " Several years ago, Russell Luepker, a professor of epidemiology at the school of public health, sought reimbursement for a $12 parking bill. The form went from a secretary to the head of his department to an accountant who entered it in a computer to a senior accountant responsible for approving it. Richard Portnoy, chief administrative officer in the epidemiology department, estimates it cost $75 to move the paperwork. When Dr. Luepker heard of it, he stopped filing for parking reimbursements. "
>
> – Douglas Belkin and Scott Thurm, The Wall Street Journal

Think about this for a second: What kind of real world skills are you going to learn in a place that can't even process its own paperwork? Most colleges and universities are like this. They're filled with bureaucratic goop. How can they survive with so much red tape? It's simple. They can be so inefficient because they have a steady "crop" of young people coming to campus each year paying huge amounts of money. And as the number of students rise, the red tape gets stickier!

Are administrators corrupt?

> The College of DuPage managed to hide more than $95 million in expenditures on more than 82,600 transactions since 2009 thanks to a peculiar type of accounting that allowed for thousands of purchases to be lumped together into one line item [...]$243,305 was spent purchasing wine and other alcohol [...] The liquor was described in an accounting ledger as 'instructional supplies.'
>
> – Drew Johnson, The Washington Times

Sometimes administrators can be corrupt. That's bad. What's worse is that you're paying these guys' salaries with your borrowed tuition money – or your parents' hard-earned savings. Not every college administration is outrageously out-of-control. But think about it for a second: Even if your prospective college is 1/10th as bad, isn't that still too bad?

The Bricks and the Mortar

It seems that colleges are constantly building new buildings – even though many schools are in debt. Why more bricks? Why more mortar?

> 66 The 'Edifice Complex' pervading higher education flies in the face of other trends that call for caution in capital spending. 99
>
> – Richard K. Vedder, Center for College Affordability and Productivity

There is a super-easy answer here: Buildings are safe. Lawns are *safe*. Parking lots are *safe*. They don't cause trouble. They don't rile up the donors. (Or the students.) They don't make insecure administrators nervous. Bricks and mortar also offer the benefit of "showcase spending." College management can point to a new building and say, "Look at this *progress!*" It's much harder to say that about faculty, research funds, or scholarships. The truth is that some of the higher powers in higher education think that buildings are easier to manage – and are more important – than people.

I've never seen so many people working out in style. What's the deal with all the fancy new gyms on college campuses?

> Today, no college tour is complete without a visit to the school's state-of-the art recreational facility. A cross between adventure park and country club, these facilities come complete with Olympic size pool...track...monster weight room...basketball, racquetball, squash, tennis, and volleyball courts galore...aerobics facilities...saunas...Jacuzzis...recumbent bikes – even a lazy river ran through one Midwest facility. And you can't have a rec-center today without a rock-climbing wall. When did America's youth develop this obsession with climbing walls? Are we preparing for war with Switzerland? Or do we want to work for Carnival Cruise Lines?
>
> – Steve Cohen, Forbes

This is important. College is not only about educating you. It can also be about making you feel like you're on vacation from reality. "High school was hard, but now it's time to play!" These fitness facilities are designed to entice, to intrigue, and to titillate. They are *not* designed to educate. Think about it: Why go to college to learn something when you can be the star of your very own four-year-long Abercrombie ad instead? Think the bricks and the mortar are your friends?

Building all these new buildings comes with a big price tag. Is that initial sticker price the final cost of the building? Or is there more? And how do those extra costs affect me?

> " New campus buildings are 'the gifts that keep on taking.' "
>
> – Lander Medlin, Executive Vice President of APPA

Once construction is finished on a new building, the real expenses *begin*. I once had a friend who worked at a small school in Iowa. They built a glass walkway over a street and several sidewalks at the center of their campus. The original cost of the walkway was about $5.5 million. But the annual cost to heat and cool this "gerbil tube" was about $80,000, the same as if the college had hired a full-time, tenured professor. Which expenditure do you think would've been of real benefit to students?

What about sports buildings?

> College sports is a carnival of construction, as schools continue to build bigger, nicer, more state-of-the art facilities for their teams. Go around to just about any power conference campus these days, and you're likely to see as many cranes, hard hats and barrier fences around sports fields as you see students.
>
> – Brian Bennett, ESPN

Donors, communities, administrators, and coaches all *love* sports buildings. And these buildings can do some awesome things. They can generate revenue. They can build prestige. They can attract star athletes. Wanna know what they *can't* do? They can't teach you one flippin' thing. (Except maybe how to waste money.)

Some college spending is pretty extreme. Couldn't they cut a couple big banquets to save me some big cash?

> " The deep and swift reductions Cal U made in its 2012-13 budget have left some wondering if the [CU] system ought to look closer for additional budget fat in its other universities, if not to save faculty jobs, then to minimize student tuition and fee increases [...] Cal U found savings in seemingly every corner of campus, from the volume of plumbing supplies it stocks to what it spends to feed donors to the amount it pays to advertise. "
>
> – Bill Schackner, Pittsburgh Post-Gazette

As we saw when we were looking at "The Administrators," colleges and universities can be extremely wasteful. And, again, since there's big money and little accountability in most of higher education, there's no reason for the waste to stop. In fact, sometimes extra administrators are hired to address these inefficiencies. And then, when that doesn't work, *more* administrators are hired to fix *those* inefficiencies! Sure, cutting waste in higher education is possible. But it will only happen with direct, external pressure. The example above shows that it *is* possible. But you've got to demand it!

I see all these lists online like "The 25 Most Beautiful College Campuses." Why is it so important to have the most attractive campus?

66 If you ask freshmen why they chose their colleges, they usually say one of two things: Either they got a good financial aid package or they thought the campus was beautiful. 99

– Adam Gross, Ayers Saint Gross architect

The bricks and the mortar of a gorgeous campus can be incredibly seductive. This is why some colleges employ more janitors and maintenance workers than they do professors. Buildings and recruiters are part of the same system; both are designed to impress you, to wow you, to give you the ole' razzle-dazzle. The down side, of course, is that once you're in the gate *you* are the one paying out a ton of money to keep up these appearances – so that they can be used to lure the next crop of incoming students.

Every business has office supplies and maintenance costs. What kind of money are we talking about for a college's "groceries?"

66 At a typical college, payroll, and benefits might make up 60 to 70 percent of the operations budget, but purchasing constitutes the next-largest chunk: about a quarter of an institution's annual budget, spent on copy paper, toilet paper, food for the dining halls, grass seed for the quad, wrenches, fuel, beakers, and much more. 99

– Scott Carlson, The Chronicle of Higher Education

Part of your tuition will always go towards "keeping the lights on." But before you spend that money, you need to think about *how* your tuition dollars are going to be spent. As it turns out, only about 25% of a college's budget will go directly to your education. Think about it: How might you better spend your money? A trip around the world? A new computer? Some gear for an excursion into the wilderness? Art supplies? You're paying a ton for a "college education." Isn't it fair that most of *your* education dollars go to *educate* you?

Powering an entire campus must be expensive. How much do colleges pay for things like heat and water?

66 Southern Illinois University spends up to $12 million a year on various utilities for major academic buildings and another $1.5 million for ancillary facilities such as the Student Center and Student Recreation Center. And those numbers are rising. The price of coal, which SIUC uses for heating and cooling campus buildings and to generate about 15 percent of its annual electrical requirements, has risen some 30 percent during the last two years. Electricity costs are up 15 to 20 percent this year alone. 99

– Tim Crosby, SIUC website

Keeping the lights on will cost your college a ton of bank. That means that it will cost *you* a ton of bank. When you're in school, you pay for the privilege of sitting in well-lit classrooms, even if those lights and those classrooms do nothing to move you forward. Think about this: You'll only spend about sixteen hours of the week in those classrooms, less than 10% of your time a week. But those lights will stay on almost all the time. On *your* dime.

How much money am I putting into my campus's lawn?

Cost data show that conventional installation of sodded turf grasses may exceed $12,000 per acre. Planting turf grass seeds may cost in the range of $4,000 to $8,000 per acre.

– US Environmental Protection Agency

When you walk across your prospective campus with your recruiter, take a few moments to think about all that grass, and all those nicely-trimmed bushes. Think hard about what these plants are doing for you. "How is this grass going to advise me as I move my dreams forward?" Or maybe something like this: "Will that bush be ready to write me an awesome letter of recommendation some day?" Since planting a quad can cost more than a professor's annual salary, those silly questions might be more important than you think.

70

Who's paying for these pretty campuses?

> Beautification, unlike renovation, is not a capital expense. Beautifications are operating expenses, which require offsetting revenue, like tuition. The cost of that is being underwritten by the students.
>
> – John Ebersole, president of Excelsior College

Who's paying for these pretty campuses? You are, of course. And that's what this is all really about, isn't it? It's a vicious circle. In order to attract students, colleges put tons of money into their campuses. In order to put tons of money into their campuses, colleges raise the cost of tuition. When does it end? Never, unfortunately. In the meantime, fees go up and the average salary for teachers goes down while the college "leadership" looks to spend another zillion dollars on another football stadium that it doesn't need.

The Liberal Arts

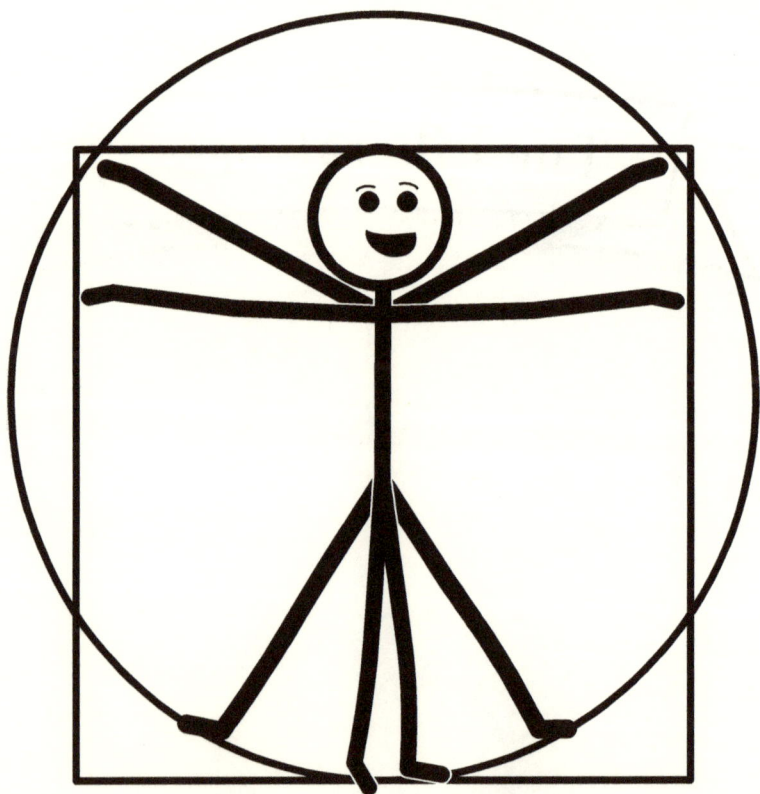

What does having a "liberal arts education" mean?

" In truth, liberal arts education no longer exists -- at least genuine liberal arts education -- in this country. We have professionalized liberal arts to the point where they no longer provide the breadth of application and the enhanced capacity for civic engagement that is their signature. Over the past century, the expert has dethroned the educated generalist to become the sole model of intellectual accomplishment. **"**

– Liz Coleman, TED2009

A "liberal arts education" doesn't mean too much, anymore. The liberal arts used to be about training the next generation of leaders to think outside the box, to provide a moral compass for Western business communities, and to advance the nobility of the human race. Now, a "liberal arts education" is more like an expensive luxury, like heated leather seats in your car: they keep your butt warm, some of the cool kids might have them, but they can't get you anywhere on their own. With the rise of the internet, a person who "knows a lot about many things" is no longer all that special. (Authentic expertise, however, will always be extremely valuable.) It's cool to know a little bit about Hegel. And astronomy. And the American civil war. And postmodern literature. Those, and a green apron, will get you a job at Starbucks.

I've heard a lot about how liberal arts majors are jobless. How do I study what I love and manage to get a job?

66 [...] I'm not suggesting we get rid of liberal arts departments – I'm suggesting we create more employable English and film majors. 'Well-rounded' and 'self-sufficient' shouldn't be mutually exclusive concepts, and combining experiential learning with access to business role models and public/private partnerships can fundamentally transform the way we think about workforce development. 99

    – Scott Gerber, founder of the Young Entrepreneur Council

Ask your recruiter – point blank – what kind of internships, co-ops, partnerships, and real world experiences your prospective college provides. Demand concrete, documented answers. If your recruiter can't provide them, then ask his or her boss. Get it all in writing. And if you don't see these opportunities on your new campus when you arrive, then leave. (Or sue.) In the end, your own initiative and your own drive will land you your first job. Your college must provide you with the real world opportunities that you need to hone those aspects of your character.

Liberal arts schools generally have a "common core."
Is this "core curriculum" really going to teach me
what I need to be a "well-rounded" person?

66 [In many liberal arts institutions] students are free to pursue 99
their own itinerary of essential knowledge. Many students satisfy
"distribution requirements" with uninspired survey courses or
with courses too esoteric or peripheral to rate as essential. At
the University of Maryland, for example, students may satisfy
their Social Sciences and History requirement with courses on
the history of sexuality, advertising, or sports.

    – Daniel de Vise, Washington Post

The "common cores," or "core curricula," at many
colleges are rooted in archaic conventions regarding
what a "well-educated person should know." The
curricula of common cores have little to do with
"reality" and – more and more often – are nothing
more than a menu of fun, "sanctioned" electives
meant to appeal to student-customers (on one hand)
and board members (on the other.) You need to ask
yourself whether or not taking eight to ten classes in
fields that you don't care about is worth the money.
Maybe it is. Maybe it isn't. But it's *your* choice,
nobody else's.

I have a feeling I can make *philosophy* work out as a career. I really love it. Should I keep on with it?

66 Of course, everyone wants to make a living out of what they love. No one wants to be disgruntled, but maybe we are setting ourselves up for just that by desiring to pursue interests that aren't jobs. We spent so much money and time cultivating those interests. They would seem to be going to waste in a cubicle, but aren't they going to waste in a coffee shop too? 99

– Maura Pennington, Forbes

In rare cases, philosophy *can* be a career. But don't think for a second that going to college means you'll be able to turn your passion for philosophy (or ceramics, or chemistry, or archaeology, or whatever) into a job. Passion is called "passion" for a reason. If you're going to follow your heart, then follow it. Don't follow a college recruiter into life-long debt and a worthless degree that will do *nothing* to move your particular interests forward. You don't need a college degree to be a philosopher. You need passion. And passion is free.

If a "well-rounded" candidate is a better job candidate, then wouldn't a liberal arts education always be the clear choice for the job market?

> 66 Elites frown upon apprenticeship programs because they think college is the way to create a 'well-rounded citizenry.' So take a look at the students in Finland, Sweden, or Germany. Are they not 'well rounded'? The argument that college creates a well-rounded citizen can be sustained only by defining 'well rounded' in a narrow way. Is someone who can quote from the school of Zen well rounded? Only if they can also maintain a motorcycle. Well-roundedness comes not from sitting in a classroom but from experiencing the larger world. 99
>
> – Alex Tabarrok, George Mason University

Being "well-rounded" comes from your adventures in the *world*. That's a fact. But colleges have everyone convinced that the opposite is true. Pretty interesting racket, don't you think? Colleges have persuaded you that *you* need *them* to become "well-rounded." But what you really need is a sense of adventure, a sense of play, a sense of humor, and a sense of the possibilities. Think about it: Why pay $45,000 a year to get what you can get for free (or almost free) by taking on a cool project, finding a mentor in a field that fascinates you, volunteering with a local organization, exploring the world, or thinking for yourself?

It doesn't seem like liberal arts schools focus too much on technology. With today's innovation, don't we need workers trained for the technologies of the future? Isn't "the future" why I'm going to college?

> 66 But to compete – and succeed – in today's global economy, our universities must do more than simply impart knowledge. They need to offer specialized courses of study that teach students how to create knowledge, innovate, and blend multiple disciplines to forge new pathways in science and technology. 99
>
> – Robert E. Geer, University at Albany-SUNY

Most liberal arts colleges have a bad track record when it comes to innovation and technology. Partly, this is because they're grounded in the "classics." In other words, the curricula of many liberal arts colleges are based on the belief that there is an unchanging "core of essential knowledge" that lies at the root of human value. This means that future-focused disciplines (like computer science, industrial design, or web development) are rarely seen as important parts of a liberal arts campus. Indeed, as they are currently taught, most of the "liberal arts" are about the past, not about the future.

How prepared will I be when I enter the job market as a "well-rounded" and "liberally-educated" individual?

> 66 When I was an undergrad, it seemed whenever I mentioned my job-search anxieties, my professors and advisors would get a glassy look in their eyes and mutter something about the career center. Their gazes would drift toward their bookshelves or a folder of ungraded papers. And at the time, I could hardly blame them. These were people who'd published dissertations on Freud, written definitive volumes on Virginia Woolf. The language of real-world career preparation was a language they simply didn't speak. 99
>
> – Kim Brooks, Salon

Another problem with the liberal arts is that they routinely discourage "career preparation." There are (at least) two reasons for this. First: Liberal arts colleges were originally set up for the rich. This means that there was no need for "career preparation," since students were at college to connect with other rich kids, to become "well-rounded," or to marry well. Second: Current liberal arts colleges actively frown upon preparing students for the job market. Faculty at many liberal arts colleges will say that their job is to "challenge you," to "inspire you," or to "expose you to the western tradition." They will very rarely say that they are there to help you find work. And that's actually a good thing, because they *can't* help you find work anyway.

If I want to go to a liberal arts college, then do I have to take courses from every single subject area?

66 Computer Science majors will find that they are taking history, political science, and geology courses along with their major's requirements. English majors will find that they have to enroll in some quantitative reasoning courses in addition to taking their literature and writing classes. Thinking they are free from the rigors of high school classes that they found boring and uninteresting, college freshmen will soon realize that they will be now be taking the advanced versions of those courses that they abhorred. 99

– Chuck Cohn, CEO of Varsity Tutors

If you go to a liberal arts college, then you'll take some classes that you might think are useless, pointless, or meaningless. Some of them will be horrible. Some of them will be great. The point is that you *must* take these courses, regardless of whether or not they're of interest or use to you. That's one of the points of the liberal arts. So think about that before you put down your hard-earned loot.

How do professors manage the broad curricula required by liberal arts colleges?

" I teach courses on IR theory, international security, regional conflict, American foreign policy, human rights, and human rights advocacy and fill in with courses on international organization, international law, and methods when needed. Prepping and maintaining courses across such breadth is great fun, but it does sacrifice depth and it does consume a lot of time that might otherwise be used for research. "

– Jon Western, Mount Holyoke College

How do teachers teach all these different courses? Easy. They water them down. Plain and simple. Since you're being trained across multiple disciplines, there's simply no time to get into the particulars. Which calls into question the idea of "training" to begin with, doesn't it? One thing that's awesome about the liberal arts is that you get to touch a tiny, little bit on *everything*. One thing that is horrible about the liberal arts is that you get to touch a *tiny*, *little* bit on everything.

So, I know that liberal arts schools are supposed to prepare me to articulate my opinions and to engage in meaningful conversation and debate. Can they deliver?

> " Far from preparing students for vigorous debate and giving them the intellectual courage to pursue truth wherever it may lead, they all too often suppress free speech and free inquiry. Of the colleges and universities in this report, not a single one merited a 'green light' rating from the Foundation for Individual Rights in Education, meaning no interference with freedom of speech and expression. Instead, 14 earned a 'red light' warning for substantial restrictions of free speech and another 11 have received a 'yellow light' warning for restrictions that jeopardize free expression. "
>
> – American Council of Trustees and Alumni, "Education or Reputation? A Look at America's Top-Ranked Liberal Arts Colleges"

Will the liberal arts help you articulate your own vision? The short answer: Not really. As it's been shown time and time again, higher education is often more about *branding* and *conformity* than training you into the sacred mysteries of "freedom and citizenship." This is a pity, because if there's one place in the world where you want to have an open exchange of ideas, then it's at college. Unfortunately, vested political interests, academic fads, and insecure administrators are terrified of what a truly open and rigorous exchange of ideas can entail. And that's why these "debates" are often confined to the bubbles of college campuses.

The Brainwash

My mom went to college, my brother went to college, and all my friends are definitely going to college. Why *wouldn't* I go?

66 We need to see college as a choice, not a requisite. Social norms dictate that we all need to go to college – but if you look through history, how many times have social norms steered us in the wrong direction? 99

    –   Dale J. Stephens, founder of UnCollege

Going to college can be amazing. But there are literally thousands of other amazing things that you can do with your life. An important thing to understand about going to college is that it's a *decision* to go to college. One of the most important things that you can ever learn about yourself is that you're in charge of your own path. Going to college is a big decision. Treat it like that – *a choice*.

82

I really have no idea why I *want* to go to college. College will give me that direction and purpose, right? Won't they teach me why I'm there when I get there?

66 The [higher education] system manufactures students who are smart and talented and driven, yes, but also anxious, timid, and lost, with little intellectual curiosity and a stunted sense of purpose: trapped in a bubble of privilege, heading meekly in the same direction, great at what they're doing but with no idea why they're doing it. 99

>   – William Deresiewicz, Excellent Sheep: The Miseducation of the American Elite and the Way to a Meaningful Life

If you don't know why you "want to go to college" now, then that's OK. You have time. In fact, if you're reading this book, then you have more than that: You've got a chance to become truly successful. Because this book is about this critical question: *Do you have the guts to think* hard *for yourself now, this moment, on one of the most important decisions of your life?* Yes? Or no? It's as simple as that.

83

I need to go to a traditional four-year university to get a "quality" education, don't I? There are no other choices out there, right?

66 I took classes by mail from the University of Washington, the University of Wyoming, and other schools with the lowest-priced correspondence courses I could find. My degree required the same number of credits and type of classes that any student at a traditional university would take... But I never met a teacher, never sat in a classroom, and to this day have never laid eyes on my beloved alma mater... And the whole degree, including the third-hand books and a sticker for the car, cost me about $10,000 in today's dollars... Did I earn a worthless degree? Hardly. My undergraduate years may have been bereft of frissons, but I wound up with a career as a tenured professor at Syracuse University, a traditional university. I am now the president of a Washington research organization. 99

– Arthur C. Brooks, American Enterprise Institute

Take a long look at Dr. Brooks' remarks. He wasn't afraid to decide for himself, to do what he wanted, and to take a chance. The question is this: *What kind of person do you really want to be?* Do you want to be someone who needs a stamp to show the world that you are "good," or "smart," or "qualified?" Or do you want to *be* good, smart, and qualified? College can be a leap forward. Or it can be a step back. If you can honestly decide for yourself what you actually "need," then you're already smarter than most college graduates.

Everyone says that I need to pick the "perfect school." That single choice affects the rest of my life, doesn't it?

> 66 The one thing that nobody ever mentions when you're initially picking a school is that you can always change your mind. Choosing a college isn't like getting a tattoo on your face...it's by no means permanent. Sure, it's no walk in the park to transfer, but you can always correct your mistake if you felt you made one. Think of it like this: If you make a wrong turn while driving, you reroute yourself, right? Nobody in their right mind would tell you to stay on the wrong road only to get yourself even more lost. For some reason, there seems to be a sort of stigma attached to transferring schools– like if you transfer, you failed. 99
>
> – Emily Grier, USA Today

Choosing the right college – if you choose college – does affect your life. But it's not the last decision that you'll ever make. And hopefully, you'll have the courage to act if it turns out that you've made the wrong choice. Once you're in the "college pipeline," you'll find it hard to get out. Most colleges are counting on your early connection to other students and the newness of the experience to do their retention work for them. But you don't have to ride that pipe all the way to the sewer. *You can leave any time that you like.* Think about it: Colleges need you. You do *not* need them. If you think that you want to go college, then make a choice, try it on, and if it's not working, then move on.

It seems like every high school wants to prepare you for one type of school: the four-year college. But what about trade schools? Do I have to pursue a "traditional" college degree?

> And rather than pushing students to attend a four-year, brick-and-mortar college in pursuit of the BA, how about business-backed training and apprenticeship programs leading to a high-skill technical degree just like in Germany and some other northern European nations? [...] In the United States, we graduate fewer students from high school, but nearly two-thirds of those we graduate go to college. More education for all. But not college for all.
>
> – James Pethokoukis, AEIdeas

Education has many forms. It always has. There are people who educate themselves. There are people who have learned everything they know from YouTube. There are people who have taken community education classes their whole lives. There are people who are *in* college their whole lives. The possibilities are endless. And that's what "choice" means. It means that you can choose for yourself what "being educated" looks like.

Won't my professors teach me the things that are important for me to know when I get to college? Isn't it their job to "open doors" for me? Won't they help me find my path?

> Faculty determine students' taste for academic fields by acting as gatekeepers, either by welcoming them into an area of knowledge, encouraging and inspiring them to explore it, or by raising the costs of entry so high so as to effectively prohibit continuing in it. Faculty can positively or negatively influence student taste for a field -- some compelling teachers can get students engaged in fields that they previously disliked, while other, more uncharismatic faculty can alienate students from entire bodies of knowledge, sometimes permanently.
>
> – Christopher G. Takacs and Daniel F. Chambliss, authors of How College Works

Finding a mentor in college is a risk – like buying a lottery ticket. You might find some amazing teachers who can teach you some amazing things. Then again, you might be taught by a pack of overworked, underpaid adjuncts. The questions you have to ask yourself at the beginning of your college search are these: "Who inspires me by example?" "Who has done the things that I want to do?" "Who has the experience to push me down the road that I've chosen for myself?" "Who can help me define – or redefine – that path for myself?" Make sure, during your campus visits, you are meeting the professors who can answer these questions for you.

Everyone at my high school has chosen a college to go to. Why should I do something different?

" Don't question these artificial societal constructs. Don't question anything. College is normal, you should want to be normal. Don't strive to be an exception. Don't attempt to break any mold or venture outside the box in which you've been placed. Some have made this grievous error, and they've all become failures, bums, terrorists, and cab drivers. "

    – Matt Walsh, The Matt Walsh Blog

Why should you do something that's different? Better question: Why should you do something that is the *same*? Hopefully, since you're reading this book, you're already self-aware enough to realize that you have choices. Maybe college is exactly what you need. Maybe it's not. The point is that it's *your* decision, so it can't be about what everyone *else* needs. It's about what *you* need.

Don't most jobs require a college degree?

> **❝** A recent report by the McKinsey Global Institute found that while low-skill jobs are on the decline, by 2020 employers around the globe will need an estimated 45 million more mid-level workers who have a high school education and vocational training. **❞**
>
> – Jenna Goudreau, Forbes

Some jobs require a college education. Some don't. In some jobs, you'll use your degree. In others, you won't. More and more employers are looking for real world experiences from their new hires. Even more importantly, many employers are looking for people who can simply do the job and do it right. You don't need a degree for that.

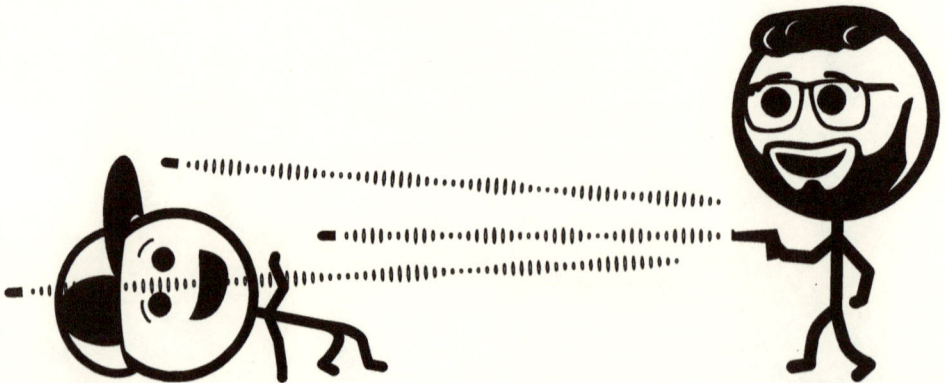

Won't college help me discover myself? Shouldn't I go to college so that I can figure out who I am and where I want to go in life?

> 66 College is a sandbox that gives you a false sense of reality. It's much more beneficial to learn what it means to direct your own life. 99
>
> – Dale J. Stephens, founder of UnCollege

College can help you discover some things, sure. But in many ways, college is also like a dream. Or, even better, it's like *The Matrix*. It seems real, but once you're out, you realize that there is a whole new world out there waiting for you. That new world is reality. College is the dream. And if you think the *dream world* can magically help you figure out who you *really* are, then you may be disappointed.

Isn't college the only way I can be considered truly educated? I should really go to school so that I can know my stuff, right?

66 Education isn't a four-year program. It's a mind-set. 99

– Benjamin Goering, Livefyre

Education is an adventure. Education is a lifestyle. Education demands creativity, passion, courage, and a willingness to humble yourself in front of reality. Education can be surreal, transcendent, and terrifying. Education is like a worm-hole into another galaxy. Education can happen anywhere and at any time. Education is a road to human nobility. Education *can* happen at college. But it doesn't *have* to.

The Deal Breakers

Tenure is disappearing for professors.

66 Since 1975, tenure and tenure-track professors have gone from roughly 45 percent of all teaching staff to less than a quarter. 99

    –   Jordan Weissmann, The Atlantic

The full-time people that do the actual teaching in college are *vanishing*. They're leaving, they're retiring, and they're not being replaced. This is a fact. But it will be rarely mentioned when you're being recruited. So you need to find out how many "tenure" or "tenure-track" faculty your prospective college employs. If it's less than 30%, then you know, without doubt, that you're going to be taught by hard-working, but underpaid adjuncts or teaching assistants. Why spend the money for that? If you're paying big dollars to go to an "elite" college, then don't you deserve to be taught by the very best and the very brightest?

The cost of attending college is unmanageable.

> The average sticker price, with room and board included, for undergraduate students attending a four-year college or university in their home state was $18,943. Out-of-state students at those schools paid, on average, $32,762. At two-year public schools, in-state students paid an average $11,052. The cost to attend a private, four-year nonprofit college: $42,419, on average, including housing and meal plan.

     – The College Board

The cost of a college degree is rising. This rise will continue. All the while, the "product" that you're buying will not noticeably improve – by any measure. If you drop $80,000 on four years of college, and if you don't work full-time during those four years, then your college degree will cost you about $80,000 in tuition and $100,000 in lost income. That doesn't include any interest, gas money, or supplies. $180,000 for four years of college is just too much.

The student debt crisis is really, really bad.

> ❝ We have more than \$1.2 trillion of student loan debt. About 10 million federal student loans are taken out annually, and then there are the insanely dangerous private student loans on top of that staggering number. And while 6.7 million borrowers in repayment mode are delinquent, the sad fact is that many lenders aren't exactly incentivized to work with borrowers. Unlike all other forms of debt, student loans can't be discharged in bankruptcy. Moreover, lenders can garnish wages and even Social Security benefits to get repaid. ❞
>
> – Suze Orman, CNBC

Not only are full-time teachers becoming more rare, and not only is the entire college experience getting more expensive, but it's also becoming more and more tied to loans. You can never, *ever* get rid of the debt that you incur as a student. Student loans can't be released by bankruptcy. So if you're thinking that you "must" go to college, then you need to stop and think again. Take another read through this little book. College is a *choice*. Make sure that massive loan repayment – which you'll carry for decades – is worth it.

College campuses are not safe. And they are getting worse.

66 Every 21 hours there is a rape on an American college campus. 99

    – National College Health Risk Behavior Survey

Over half the violent attacks on college campuses this past century have happened in the past 20 years.

    – "Campus Attacks", study from Secret Service, FBI, U.S. Department of Education

Think all that money and all those loans are going to buy you a safe haven from the insanity of the "real world?" Think again. Never in our history has higher education been more dangerous. Get the safety statistics of your prospective campus from your recruiter. If he or she can't give them to you, then get them from the campus security director. Review them carefully. Remember: You are paying for an *education*. You aren't paying to get hazed, assaulted, or abused. If your campus isn't safe, then should you be calling it "your" campus?

95

Going to college will not get you a stellar job.

" The number of college graduates working minimum wage jobs is nearly 71 percent higher than it was a decade ago, according to the Bureau of Labor Statistics' latest figures. "

– Danielle Kurtzleben, U.S. News

Getting a college degree doesn't automatically equal work. In fact, if that's what you're looking for – an easy road towards full-time employment – then you're in for a rude awakening. The business leaders, the creatives, and the innovators of tomorrow aren't looking for someone who has the "right degree" or someone who has "good grades." They're looking for someone who's smart, someone who's hungry, and – above all – someone who can think for themself. In the next twenty years, having a college degree may even be a mark *against* you. Unless you can prove yourself with real work, through real projects, and in real life, your dream job may forever be out of reach. College can't guarantee employment. That's a fact.

The One Reason

So, I've gone through some reasons why you might not want to go to college. But what about the reasons to go? Aren't there tons of those? Sure. But the most important – by far – is this: the people.

The people that you meet in college will change your life. They'll become a part of your new reality. They'll affect who you are, who you become, and who you think you can be. They'll challenge you, confront you, support you, and love you. They'll force you to examine your values, your strengths, your weaknesses, and your world. (And – of course – you'll affect them in turn.) The people are what it's all about.

Nowhere, outside of college, will you find a similar sphere for connecting, networking, and transforming your immediate peer group. You'll be on your own for the first time. The stakes will be high. And with this new environment will come a new kind of intensity in your personal relationships. You may remember your high school buddies. But you'll never forget your college friends. Your best high school teachers may keep a little place in your heart. But your college professors will live large in your mind for the rest of your life. Your memories of high school may be nice. But your college memories will become the stuff of legend! For making new friends, climbing the networking ladder, and expanding your social world, nothing can beat going to college.

It's this amazing, unforgettable social aspect of college – the people – that will always make college great. Indeed, this aspect of the college experience is nearly impossible to duplicate through other kinds of educational experiences or other kinds of adventures. So, if there is one reason to go to college, then this is it.

Does this mean that you "must" go to college? Hardly. But it does mean that you've got a big decision ahead of you. You can do it. It's your life. You are in charge. You can do anything you want! Good luck!

Bibliography

Chapter One – The Money

Odland, Steve. "College Costs Out Of Control." Entrepeneurs. *Forbes*, March 24, 2012. http://www.forbes.com/sites/steveodland/2012/03/24/college-costs-are-soaring/.

Davidson, Jacob. "3 Mistakes That Will Cost You a College Scholarship." Money. *Time*, September 3, 2014. http://time.com/money/3149027/dont-lose-your-college-scholarship/

Kantrowitz, Barbara. "Getting Into College – and Paying For It: A Teen's First Adult Decision." Higher Ed. *Hechinger Report*, March 12, 2014. http://hechingerreport.org/content/getting-college-paying-teens-first-adult-decision_15112/

Marcus, Jon. "College Enrollment Shows Signs of Slowing." Higher Ed. *Hechinger Report*, May 31, 2012. http://hechingerreport.org/content/college-enrollment-shows-signs-of-slowing_8688/

Cohen, Steve. "A Quick Way to Cut College Costs." *New York Times*, March 20, 2014. http://www.nytimes.com/2014/03/21/opinion/a-quick-way-to-cut-college-costs.html?_r=0

FinAid. "Tuition Inflation." http://www.finaid.org/savings/tuition-inflation.phtml

Moore, Carole. "Surprise! College Costs Even More." *Bankrate,* August 15, 2011. http://www.bankrate.com/finance/personal-finance/surprise-college-costs-even-more-than-you-thought-1.aspx

Bowyer, Chris. "Student Loan Interest: Compounding the Problem." *Forbes*, March 14, 2014. http://www.forbes.com/sites/thecollegebubble/2014/03/14/student-loan-interest-compounding-the-problem/

Swidey, Neil. "The Four-Year College Myth." *Boston Globe*, May 31, 2009. http://www.boston.com/news/education/higher/articles/2009/05/31/the_four_year_college_myth/

Desrochers, Donna M., et.al. "Trends In College Spending 1998-2008: Where Does the Money Come From? Where Does it Go? What Does it Buy?" Washington, D.C.: American Institutes for Research. 2010.

Chapter Two – The Recruiters

U.S. Congress. *Congressional Record.* 112th Cong., 1st sess., 2011. Vol. 157, pt. 18.

Kirkham, Chris. "With Goldman's Foray Into Higher Educaion, A Predatory Pursuit of Students and Revenues." HuffPost Business. *Huffington Post,* October 14, 2011. http://www.huffingtonpost. com/2011/10/14/goldman-sachs-for-profit-college_n_997409.html

Cohen, Steve. "The Out-of-State Admissions Edge." *The Daily Beast,* August 18, 2011. http://www.thedailybeast.com/articles/2011/08/18/ college-admissions-which-state-schools-give-an-edge-to-out-of-state-students.html

Popper, Nathaniel. "Committing to Play for a College, Then Starting 9th Grade." *New York Times,* January 26, 2014. http://www.nytimes. com/2014/01/27/sports/committing-to-play-for-a-college-then-starting-9th-grade.html

Cohen, Steve. "The Three Biggest Lies in College Admission." *Forbes,* September 29, 2012. http://www.forbes.com/sites/ stevecohen/2012/09/29/the-three-biggest-lies-in-college-admission/2/?commentId=comment_blogAndPostId/blog/comment/1098-285-189

Marshall, Jack. "College Admissions Diversity Deception, Student Ethics Corruption." *Ethics Alarms* (blog), January 1, 2014. http:// ethicsalarms.com/2014/01/01/college-admissions-diversity-deception-student-ethics-corruption/

Chace, William M. "Stress Test: Why the College Admissions Process Is So Nerve-Wracking." *The American Interest,* December 12, 2012. http://www.the-american-interest.com/2012/12/12/stress-test-why-the-college-admissions-process-is-so-nerve-wracking/

Schwartz, Katrina. "Do Rigid College Admissions Leave Room for Creative Thinkers?" *MindShift* (blog), January 10, 2014. http:// blogs.kqed.org/mindshift/2014/01/do-rigid-college-admissions-leave-room-for-creative-thinkers/

Godfrey, Steven. "Meet the Bag Man." *SBNation,* April 10, 2014. http://www.sbnation.com/college-football/2014/4/10/5594348/ college-football-bag-man-interview

Smith, Tovia. "Colleges Work Harder to Lure New Students." *Morning Edition.* NPR. Podcast audio, March 30, 2009. http://www.npr.org/ templates/story/story.php?storyId=102451618

Chapter 3 – The Student-Athlete

LeMay, Joey. "March Madness: The Debate to Pay Poor College Athletes Continues as Institutions Gain Billions." *MintPress News*, March 19, 2012. http://www.mintpressnews.com/should-ncaa-pay -student-athletes-most-live-below-federal-poverty-line/22421/

Fecke, Jeff. "Nine Football Players Killed By Brain Trauma." *Truthout*, February 3, 2013. http://truth-out.org/news/item/14314-9-football-players-killed-by-brain-trauma

Williams, Mary Elizabeth. "Why Do We Fumble Over Athletes and Rape Accusations?" *Salon*, April 16, 2014. http://www.salon.com/2014/04/16/why_do_we_fumble_over_athletes_and_rape_accusations/

National Eating Disorders Association. *Coach and Athletic Trainer Toolkit*. 2010. http://www.nationaleatingdisorders.org/coach-trainer

Ganim, Sara. "CNN Analysis: Some College Athletes Play Like Adults, Read Like 5th-Graders." *CNN*, January 8, 2014. http://www.cnn.com/2014/01/07/us/ncaa-athletes-reading-scores/

Johnson, Greg, and StudentNation. "The NCAA Makes Billions and Student Athletes Get None of It." *StudentNation* (blog), April 9, 2014. http://www.thenation.com/blog/179272/ncaa-makes-billions-and-student-athletes-get-none-it#

Branch, Taylor. "The Shame of College Sports." *The Atlantic*, September 7, 2011. http://www.theatlantic.com/magazine/archive/2011/10/the-shame-of-college-sports/308643/?single_page=true

Zirin, Dave. "The NCAA: Poster Boy for Corruption and Exploitation." *The Nation*, March 12, 2013. http://www.thenation.com/article/173307/ncaa-poster-boy-corruption-and-exploitation

Peale, Cliff. "Athletics Cost Colleges, Students Millions." *USA Today*, September 15, 2013. http://www.usatoday.com/story/news/nation/2013/09/15/athletics-cost-colleges-students-millions/2814455/

Goodman, Joseph. "What's the Source of Football's Continuing Corruption? Undeterred Fans and Their Money." *Miami Herald*, September 13, 2013. http://www.miamiherald.com/sports/article1954923.html

Newlon, Cara. "The College Amenities Arms Race." *Forbes*, July 31, 2014. http://www.forbes.com/sites/caranewlon/2014/07/31/the-college-amenities-arms-race/

Segal, Matthew. "The Big College Ranking Sham: Why You Must Ignore U.S. News and World's Report List." *Salon*, September 15, 2014. http://www.salon.com/2014/09/15/the_big_college_ranking_sham_why_you_must_ignore_u_s_news_and_worlds_report_list/

Romeo, Nick. "How to Reinvent College." *Daily Beast*, May 13, 2013. http://www.thedailybeast.com/articles/2013/05/13/how-to-reinvent-college.html

Hoeller, Sophie-Claire. "10 College Amenities So Insane You'll Want to go Back to School." *Thrillist*, September 7, 2014. http://www.thrillist.com/travel/nation/colleges-with-the-best-perks-amenities-so-insane-you-ll-want-to-go-back-to-school

Wang, Marian. "On 'Country Club' Campuses: A Public University Ex-President Shares His Second Thoughts." *ProRublica*, November 11, 2013. http://www.propublica.org/article/on-country-club-campuses-a-public-university-ex-president-shares-his-second

Weinmann, Karlee. "The Ten Most Bizarre College Courses." *Business Insider*, June 22, 2011. http://www.businessinsider.com/expensive-college-courses-2011-6

Rubin, Bonnie Miller and Jodi S. Cohen. "In April, It's Colleges' Turn to Woo Students." *Chicago Tribune*, April 15, 2011. http://articles.chicagotribune.com/2011-04-15/news/ct-met-college-courtship-0416-20110415_1_top-tier-colleges-admissions-officers-new-admissions-director

Zirm, Jordan. "17 Insanely Expensive College Athletic Training Facilities." *Stack*, June 2, 2014. http://www.stack.com/2014/06/02/expensive-college-athletic-training-facilities/

Podolsky, Doug. "How Do Schools Market Themselves to Attract Students?" College of Tomorrow. *U.S. News & World Report*, September 22, 2014. http://www.usnews.com/news/college-of-tomorrow/articles/2014/09/22/how-do-schools-market-themselves-to-attract-students

Landphair, Ted. "College Dangle Perks to Attract Students." *Voice of America*, May 18, 2011. http://www.voanews.com/content/colleges-dangle-perks-to-attract-students-122233944/162729.html

Chapter 5 – The Professors

Sanchez, Claudio. "Part-Time Professors Demand Higher Pay; Will Colleges Listen?" *All Things Considered*. Podcast audio, February 3, 2014. http://www.npr.org/2014/02/03/268427156/part-time-professors-demand-higher-pay-will-colleges-listen

House Committee on Education and the Workforce. "The Just-In-Time Professor: A Staff Report Summarizing eForum Responses on the Working Conditions of Contingent Faculty in Higher Education." January 24, 2014. http://democrats.edworkforce.house.gov/sites/democrats.edworkforce.house.gov/files/documents/1.24.14-AdjunctEforumReport.pdf

Chomsky, Noam. "The Death of American Universities." *Jacobin*, March 3, 2014. https://www.jacobinmag.com/2014/03/the-death-of-american-universities/

Scott, Debra Leigh. "How American Universities Have Destroyed Scholarship in the U.S." *The Homeless Adjunct* (blog). August 6, 2014. https://junctrebellion.wordpress.com/2014/08/06/how-american-universities-have-destroyed-scholarship-in-the-u-s/

Sweet, Steve, et.al. *Who is Professor Staff? And How Can This Person Teach so Many Students?* (Center for the Future of Higher Education, Think Tank Report No. 2.) http://futureofhighered.org//wp-content/uploads/2012/08/ProfStaffFinal1.pdf

Guest Post "The Real Life of a Tenure Track Faculty Person." *The Professor Is In* (blog). April 16, 2013. http://theprofessorisin.com/2013/04/16/the-real-life-of-a-tenure-track-faculty-person/

Kezar, Adrianna, and Daniel Maxey. *The Changing Faculty and Student Success: Selected Research on Connections between Non-Tenure-Track Faculty and Student Learning.* Los Angeles: Pallias Center for Higher Education, 2012.

Adjunct Action. *The High Cost of Adjunct Living: Boston.* SEIU. http://www.seiu509.org/files/2013/12/The-High-Cost-of-Adjunct-Living-in-Boston-12113.pdf

Ginsberg, Benjamin. "Tenure and Academic Freedom: The Beginning of the End." *Academic Matters* (May 2012): 25. http://www.academicmatters.ca/assets/AcademicMatters_May12.pdf

Chapter 6 – The Administrators

Zywicki, Todd. "Administrative Bloat at Universities." *The Volokh Conspiracy* (blog). August 24, 2010. http://volokh.com/2010/08/24/administrative-bloat-at-universities/

Bennett, Daniel L. "Bureaucrat U." *Forbes,* June 26, 2009. http://www.forbes.com/forbes/2009/0713/opinions-college-tuition-teachers-on-my-mind.html

Finnie, Hannah. "The Hidden Crisis on College Campuses." *Generation Progress,* July 8, 2014. http://genprogress.org/voices/2014/07/08/28916/the-hidden-crisis-on-college-campuses/

Ginsberg, Benjamin. "Administrators Ate My Tuition." *Washington Monthly,* September-October 2011. http://www.washingtonmonthly.com/magazine/septemberoctober_2011/features/administrators_ate_my_tuition031641.php?page=all

Vedder, Richard K. "As Tuition Increases, So Do College Bureaucracies." *Bloomberg View,* February 3, 2014. http://www.bloombergview.com/articles/2014-02-03/how-many-provosts-do-colleges-need-

Reynolds, Glenn Harlan. "Beat the Tuition Bloat." *USA Today,* February 17, 2014. http://www.usatoday.com/story/opinion/2014/02/17/college-tuition-job-students-loan-debt-column/5531461/

Weissmann, Jordan. "This State College President Earned $6 Million Last Year. Should You Be Mad?" MoneyBox. *Slate,* May 20, 2014. http://www.slate.com/blogs/moneybox/2014/05/20/college_president_pay_is_it_too_high.html

Belkin, Douglas, and Scott Thurm. "Deans List: Hiring Spree Fattens College Bureaucracy – And Tuition." *Wall Street Journal,* December 28, 2012. http://www.wsj.com/articles/SB10001424127887323316804578161490716042814

Johnson, Drew. "How a College Hid $95 Million in Expense Like Booze, Shooting Clubs." *The Washington Times,* October 2, 2014. http://www.washingtontimes.com/news/2014/oct/2/golden-hammer-college-hid-95m-in-administrator-boo/?page=all

Chapter 7 – The Bricks and the Mortar

Cohen, Steve. "Oh, So That's Why College Is So Expensive." *Forbes*, August, 28, 2012. http://www.forbes.com/sites/stevecohen/2012/08/28/oh-so-thats-why-college-is-so-expensive/

Martin, Andrew. "Building a Showcase Campus, Using an I.O.U." *New York Times*, December 13, 2012. http://www.nytimes.com/2012/12/14/business/colleges-debt-falls-on-students-after-construction-binges.html?pagewanted=all&_r=0

Marcus, Jon. "Public Universities Plow Ahead with Billions in Construction Despite Tight Budgets." *Hechinger Report*, March 15, 2012. http://hechingerreport.org/public-universities-plow-ahead-with-billions-in-construction-despite-tight-budgets/

Bennett, Brian. "Arms Race Proves Recession-Proof." College Football. *ESPN*, June 14, 2012. http://espn.go.com/college-football/story/_/id/8047787/college-football-facilities-arms-race-proves-recession-proof

Schackner, Bill. "Frugal California University of Pennsylvania Cuts Back on Spending, Saves Millions." *Pittsburgh Post-Gazette*, October 7, 2013. http://www.post-gazette.com/news/education/2013/10/07/Frugal-California-University-of-Pennsylvania-cuts-back-on-spending-saves-millions/stories/201310070056

Tep, Ratha. "America's Most Beautiful College Campuses." *Travel and Leisure*, September 2011. http://www.travelandleisure.com/slideshows/americas-most-beautiful-college-campuses

Carlson, Scott. "Colleges See Big Savings in Centralized Buying." *The Chronicle of Higher Education*, April 14, 2014. http://chronicle.com/article/Colleges-See-Big-Savings-in/145879/

Crosby, Tim. "SIUC Looking High and Low to Trim Energy Costs." *Southern Illinois University News*, August 1, 2006. http://news.siu.edu/2006/08/080106tc6149.php

"Greenacres: A Source Book on Natural Landscaping for Public Officials." Prepared by the Northeastern Illinois Planning Commission. 1997. http://www.epa.gov/greenacres/toolkit/chap2.html

Whelan, Corey. "Tuition Hikes: Why Higher Education Spends Millions on Campus Cosmetics." *CBS New York*, March 27, 2013. http://newyork.cbslocal.com/2013/03/27/tuition-hikes-why-higher-education-spends-millions-on-campus-cosmetics/

Chapter 8 – The Liberal Arts

Coleman, Liz. "A Call to Reinvent Liberal Arts Education." Filmed February 2009. TED video, 18:38. http://www.ted.com/talks/liz_coleman_s_call_to_reinvent_liberal_arts_education?language=en

Gerber, Scott. "How Liberal Arts Colleges are Failing America." *The Atlantic,* September 24, 2012. http://www.theatlantic.com/business/archive/2012/09/how-liberal-arts-colleges-are-failing-america/262711/

DeVise, Daniel. "The Education Review 8 Big Ideas for Improving Higher Ed." *Washington Post Magazine*, February 20, 2011. http://www.goacta.org/news/the_education_review_8_big_ideas_for_improving_higher_ed

Pennington, Maura. "A Liberal Arts Degree Doesn't Correlate With an Easier Life." Opinion. *Forbes*, February 24, 2012. http://www.forbes.com/sites/maurapennington/2012/02/14/a-liberal-arts-degree-doesnt-correlate-with-an-easier-life/

Tabarrok, Alex. "Tuning In to Dropping Out." The Chronicle Review. *Chronicle of Higher Education*, March 4, 2012. http://chronicle.com/article/Tuning-In-to-Dropping-Out/130967/

"College Grads Need Skills, Not Liberal Arts." With contributions by Robert E. Geer and Linda H. Halisky. The Debate Room. *Bloomberg Businessweek*, May 2011. http://www.businessweek.com/debateroom/archives/2011/05/college_grads_need_skills_not_liberal_arts.html

Brooks, Kim. "Is it Time to Kill the Liberal Arts Degree?" *Salon*, June 19, 2011. http://www.salon.com/2011/06/19/time_to_kill_liberal_arts/

Cohn, Chuck. "Why You Need to Take Gen Eds and How You Can Appreciate Them." HuffPost College (blog). August 7, 2013. http://www.huffingtonpost.com/chuck-cohn/why-you-need-to-take-gen-_b_3720942.html

Western, Jon. "So You Want to be a Liberal Arts College Professor?" Duck of Minerva (blog). January 18, 2013. http://www.whiteoliphaunt.com/duckofminerva/2013/01/so-you-want-to-be-a-liberal-arts-college-professor.html

ACTA. *Education or Reputation?* American Council of Trustees and Alumni, Executive Summary, January 2014. http://www.goacta.org/executivesummary/education_or_reputation_executive_summary

Chapter 9 – The Brainwash

Stephens, Dale J. "Do You Really Have to Go to College?" The Choice (blog). *New York Times*, March 7, 2013. http://thechoice.blogs. nytimes.com/2013/03/07/do-you-really-have-to-go-to-college/

Deresiewicz, William. *Excellent Sheep: The Miseducation of the American Elite and the Way to a Meaningful Life*. New York: Free Press, 2014, quoted in Nathan Heller, "Poison Ivy." *The New Yorker,* September 1, 2014. http://www.newyorker.com/magazine/2014/09/01/poison-ivy

Brooks, Arthur C. "My Valuable, Cheap College Degree." The Opinion Pages. *New York Times*, January 31, 2013. http://www.nytimes. com/2013/02/01/opinion/my-valuable-cheap-college-degree.html

Pethokoukis, James. "Harvard, We Have a Problem: Too Many Liberal Arts Majors." *American Enterprise Institute*, March 7, 2012. http://www.aei.org/publication/harvard-we-have-a-problem-too-many-liberal-arts-majors/print/

Grier, Emily. "The Complete Collection of Lies that High School Told Me." Voices from College. *USA Today*, August 11, 2011. http:// college.usatoday.com/2011/08/11/the-complete-collection-of-lies-that-high-school-told-me/

Jaschik, Scott. "Majoring in a Professor." *Inside Higher Ed*, August 12, 2013. https://www.insidehighered.com/news/2013/08/12/study-finds-choice-major-most-influenced-quality-intro-professor

Walsh, Matt. "Kids, Go to College or You'll Die Alone in Misery." *The Matt Walsh Blog* (blog). August 23, 2013. http://themattwalshblog. com/2013/08/23/kids-go-to-college-or-youll-die-alone-in-misery/

Goudreau, Jenna. "The Best Jobs that Don't Require a Bachelor's Degree." Forbeswoman. *Forbes*, June 21, 2012. http://www.forbes. com/sites/jennagoudreau/2012/06/21/the-best-jobs-that-dont-require-a-bachelors-degree/

Ojalvo, Holly Epstein. "Why Go to College at All?" The Choice. *New York Times*, February 2, 2012. http://thechoice.blogs.nytimes. com/2012/02/02/why-go-to-college-at-all/

Williams, Alex. "Saying No to College." *New York Times*, November 30, 2012. http://www.nytimes.com/2012/12/02/fashion/saying-no-to-college.html?pagewanted=all&_r=0

The Dealbreakers

Weissmann, Jordan. "The Ever-Shrinking Role of Tenured Professors (in 1 Chart)." *The Atlantic*, April 10, 2013. http://www.theatlantic. com/business/archive/2013/04/the-ever-shrinking-role-of-tenured-college-professors-in-1-chart/274849/

Hefling, Kimberly. "College Prices Continue to Inch Higher." Newshour. *PBS*, November 13, 2014. http://www.pbs.org/newshour/ rundown/sticker-price-college-continues-inch-higher/

Orman, Suze. "Biggest Economic Threat? Student Loan Debt." *USA Today*, October 25, 2014. http://www.usatoday.com/story/money/ personalfinance/2014/10/25/student-loan-debt/17773131/

D'Angelo, Alexa. "Combatting Sexual Assault on Campus." *State Press Magazine*, October 24, 2014. http://www.statepress.com/2014/10/24/ combatting-sexual-assault-on-campus/

Nemana, Vivekananda. "Rising Trend of Violence on College Campuses." *NYULocal*, April 20, 2010. http://nyulocal.com/ national/2010/04/20/rising-trend-of-violence-on-college-campuses/

Kurtzleben, Danielle. "Twice as Many College Grads in Minimum Wage Jobs as 5 Years Ago." *U.S. News*, December 5, 2013. http:// www.usnews.com/news/articles/2013/12/05/twice-as-many-college-grads-in-minimum-wage-jobs-as-5-years-ago

Suggestions for Future Reading

Chapter 1

Brown, Meta, et.al. *Measuring Student Debt and Its Performance*. Federal Reserve Bank of New York Staff Reports, no. 668. April 2014.

Dugan, Andrew and Stephanie Kafka. "Student Debt Linked to Worse Health and Less Wealth." Gallup, August 7, 2014. http://www.gallup.com/poll/174317/student-debt-linked-worse-health-less-wealth.aspx

Desrochers, Donna M. and Steven Hurlburt. "Trends In College Spending: 2001-2011." Washington, D.C.: American Institutes for Research. 2014.

Fry, Richard. 2014. "Young Adults, Student Debt and Economic Well-Being." Washington D.C.: Pew Research Center.

Chapter 2

Collins, Mimi. "Best Practices for College Recruiting." National Association for Colleges and Employers. https://www.naceweb.org/knowledge/recruiting/college-best-practices.aspx

GAO. *For-Profit Colleges: Undercover Testing Finds Colleges Encouraged Fraud and Engaged in Deceptive and Questionable Marketing Practices.* Testimony before the Committee on Health, Education, Labor, and Pensions, U.S. Senate. 2010. http://www.propublica.org/documents/item/for-profit-college-encouraged-fraud-used-deceptive-marketing

Godfrey, Steven. "Meet the Bag Man." *SBNation*, April 10, 2014. http://www.sbnation.com/college-football/2014/4/10/5594348/college-football-bag-man-interview

Smith, Tovia. "Colleges Work Harder to Lure New Students." *Morning Edition*. NPR. Podcast audio, March 30, 2009. http://www.npr.org/templates/story/story.php?storyId=102451618

Chapter 3

Berkowitz, Steve. "Judge Releases Ruling on O'Bannon Case: NCAA Loses." *USA Today,* August 8, 2014. http://www.usatoday.com/story/sports/college/2014/08/08/ed-obannon-antitrust-lawsuit-vs-ncaa/13801277/

Ganim, Sara, and Devon Sayers. "UNC Report Finds 18 Years of Academic Fraud to Keep Athletes Playing." *CNN,* October 23, 2014. http://www.cnn.com/2014/10/22/us/unc-report-academic-fraud/index.html?hpt=hp_t1

Huma, R., and E.J. Staurowsky. "The $6 Billion Heist: Robbing College Athletes Under the Guise of Amateurism." National College Players Association and Drexel University Sport Management. 2012. http://www.ncpanow.org/news/articles/body/6-Billion-Heist-Study_Full.pdf

Huml, Matthew R., et.al. "Exploring the Role of Educational Institutions in Student-Athlete Community Engagement." Journal of Issues in Intercollegiate Athletics 7 (2014): 224-244.

Solomon, Jon. "NCAA Settlement: Football Players Carry 3 Times Risk of CTE Symptoms." *CBSSports,* July 30, 2014. http://www.cbssports.com/collegefootball/writer/jon-solomon/24643655/ncaa-settlement-football-players-carry-3-times-risk-of-cte-symptoms

Chapter 4

Jacob, Brian, et. al. "College as Country Club: Do Colleges Cater to Students' Preferences for Consumption?" No. w18745. National Bureau of Economic Research, 2013. http://www.nber.org/papers/w18745

Joseph, Matthew, et. Al. "University Branding: Understanding Students' Choice of an Educational Institution." *Journal of Brand Management* 20, no. 1 (2012): 1-12. http://www.palgrave-journals.com/bm/journal/v20/n1/abs/bm201213a.html

Kreuter, Nate. "Customer Mentality." *Insider Higher Ed,* February 27, 2014. https://www.insidehighered.com/views/2014/02/27/essay-critiques-how-student-customer-idea-erodes-key-values-higher-education

Martinez-Saenz, Miguel, and Steven Schoonover Jr. "Resisting the 'Student-as-Consumer' Metaphor." *Academe,* November-December 2014. http://www.aaup.org/article/resisting-student-consumer-metaphor#.VNfzNPnF_ts

Chapter 5

Benjamin, Ernst. "Some Implications of Tenure for the Profession and Society." *AAUP*, 1997. http://www.aaup.org/issues/tenure/some-implications-tenure-profession-and-society

The Coalition on the Academic Workforce. "A Portrait of Part-Time Faculty Members." 2012. http://www.nea.org/assets/docs/HE/neacontingentplan.pdf

Hoeller, Keith. *Equality for Contingent Faculty: Overcoming the Two-Tier System*. Nashville: Vanderbilt University Press. 2014.

House Committee on Education and the Workforce. "The Just-In-Time Professor: A Staff Report Summarizing eForum Responses on the Working Conditions of Contingent Faculty in Higher Education." January 24, 2014. http://democrats.edworkforce.house.gov/sites/democrats.edworkforce.house.gov/files/documents/1.24.14-AdjunctEforumReport.pdf

Smith, S.E. "The Disposable Professor Crisis." *Salon*, April 4, 2012. http://www.salon.com/2012/04/04/the_disposable_professor_crisis/

Chapter 6

Desrochers, Donna M., and Rita Kirshstein. "Labor Intensive or Labor Expensive? Changing Staffing and Compensation Patterns in Higher Education." Washington D.C.: American Institutes for Research, 2014. http://www.deltacostproject.org/sites/default/files/products/DeltaCostAIR_Staffing_Brief_2_3_14.pdf

Curtis, John W., and Saranna Thornton. "Losing Focus: The Annual Report on the Economic Status of the Profession, 2013-14." *Academe*, March-April 2014. http://www.aaup.org/file/zreport.pdf

Ginsberg, Benjamin. *The Fall of the Faculty: The Rise of the All-Administrative University and Why It Matters*. Oxford: Oxford University Press, 2011.

Hechinger, John. "Bureaucrats Paid $250,000 Feed Outcry Over College Costs." *BloombergBusiness*, November 13, 2012. http://www.bloomberg.com/news/articles/2012-11-14/bureaucrats-paid-250-000-feed-outcry-over-college-costs

Chapter 7

Dill, David D., and Maarja Soo. "Academic Quality, League Tables, and Public Policy: A Cross-National Analysis of University Ranking Systems." Higher Education 49, no. 4 (2005): 495-533. http://link.springer.com/article/10.1007/s10734-004-1746-8

Kadamus, Jim. "The State of Facilities in Higher Education: 2013 Benchmarks, Best Practices, & Trends." Guilford: Sightlines. 2013. http://www.sightlines.com/wp-content/uploads/2013/10/The-State-of-Facilities-in-Higher-Education-2013-Benchmarks-Best-Practices-Trends.pdf

Martin, Andrew. "Building a Showcase Campus, Using an I.O.U." The New York Times. December 13, 2012. http://www.nytimes.com/2012/12/14/business/colleges-debt-falls-on-students-after-construction-binges.html?pagewanted=all

Vedder, Richard. "Colleges' Athletics Arms Race Is For Losers." BloombergBusiness, December 27, 2013. http://www.bloomberg.com/news/articles/2013-12-27/colleges-athletics-arms-race-is-for-losers

Chapter 8

Coleman, Liz. "A call to reinvent liberal arts education." Filmed February 2009. TED video, 18:38. https://www.ted.com/talks/liz_coleman_s_call_to_reinvent_liberal_arts_education?language=en

Flores, Antoinette. "Competency-Based Education: Adding Value in the Liberal Arts." Center for American Progress, June 12, 2014. https://www.americanprogress.org/issues/higher-education/news/2014/06/12/91465/competency-based-education-adding-value-in-the-liberal-arts/

McNutt, Mark I. "There Is Value in Liberal Arts Education, Employers Say." U.S. News & World Report, September 22, 2014. http://www.usnews.com/news/college-of-tomorrow/articles/2014/09/22/there-is-value-in-liberal-arts-education-employers-say

NPR. "Amid Rising College Costs, A Defense of the Liberal Arts." All Things Considered. NPR. Podcast audio, August 3, 2014.

Chapter 9

Bachmann, Helena. "Who Needs College? The Swiss Opt for Vocational School." Time, October 4, 2012. http://world.time.com/2012/10/04/who-needs-college-the-swiss-opt-for-vocational-school/

Carnevale, Anthony P., et.al. "The College Payoff: Education, Occupations, Lifetime Earnings." Washington, D.C.: Georgetown University Center on Education and the Workforce, 2011.

Moynihan, Michael. "How 1960s Radicals Ended Up Teaching Your Kids." The Daily Beast, April 10, 2013. http://www.thedailybeast.com/articles/2013/04/10/how-1960s-radicals-ended-up-teaching-your-kids.html

Price, Michael. "7 Reasons You Shouldn't Go to College and 4 Things to Do Instead." HuffPost Business, June 17, 2014. http://www.huffingtonpost.com/michaelprice/7-reasons-why-you-shouldn_1_b_5501111.html

pedro degrasi is a sociologist, entrepreneur, and adventurer. He grew up in Texas, but now lives between New York, Amsterdam, and Buenos Aires. When not writing in his areas of interest – education, religion, technology, design, and the environment – he enjoys reading Jung, Rand, Marx, and Rilke.

www.ingramcontent.com/pod-product-compliance
Lightning Source LLC
Chambersburg PA
CBHW030715110426
42739CB00030B/437